THE MAGNET EFFECT

DESIGNING OUTREACH EVENTS THAT DRAW KIDS TO CHRIST

BARRY ST. CLAIR

VICTOR BOOKS

A DIVISION OF SCRIPTURE PRESS PUBLICATIONS INC.
USA CANADA ENGLAND

Also Available from Barry St. Clair:

Penetrating the Campus: Reaching Kids Where They Are

Taking Your Campus for Christ

The Love, Sex, and Dating Series

The Moving Toward Maturity Series

   Following Jesus

   Spending Time Alone with God

   Making Jesus Lord

   Giving Away Your Faith

   Influencing Your World

Unless otherwise indicated, Scripture taken from the HOLY BIBLE, NEW INTERNATIONAL VERSION. Copyright © 1973, 1978, 1984 by International Bible Society. Used by permission of Zondervan Publishing House. All rights reserved.

The "NIV" and "New International Version" trademarks are registered in the United States Patent and Trademark Office by International Bible Society. Use of either trademark requires the permission of International Bible Society.

ISBN 1-56476-352-8

Cover Design: Joe DeLeon

2 3 4 5 6 7 8 9 10

Printing/Year 97 96 95 94

Produced for Victor Books by The Livingstone Corporation. David R. Veerman, J. Michael Kendrick, and Brenda James Todd, project staff. Printed in the United States of America

*To the men who lovingly and patiently hold me accountable
for my life, family and ministry.*

Howard St.Clair—my Dad

Buddy Price

Brad Leeper

Sonny Davis

John Howard

David Scott

Jim Underwood

Bill Williams

*Without your ministry to me I would be
incomplete in my ministry to others.*

WHO DESERVES CREDIT FOR THIS BOOK?

Writing a book becomes a mind-numbing, body-exhausting, spirit-depleting experience, especially when the deadline is starring you down. When I get to that critical point it takes total, absolute, all-consuming focus. Not only do I pay a price, but those who live with me every day have to endure me. Thanks, Carol dear, for loving me when I was cross and grouchy and should have been giving my attention to you. And to my kids who let me take part of my vacation to finish this. And to my staff at Reach Out Ministries who have covered for me in my absence.

Writing a book also becomes a team effort. On this particular one I've had help from some people who co-labor with me in youth ministry. They inspired me because they practice with excellence what I wrote in this book. They encourage me because they supplied ideas, information and illustrations for this book. They motivate me because of their long-term commitment to fulfill the Great Commission among the younger generation. Thanks, my good and faithful brothers.

Rick Caldwell	Sam Davis
Matt Brinkley	Mike Ennis
Roger Palmer	Billy Lord
Jeff Hodges	Steve Parr
Alan Daniels	Charlie Weir
Lanny Donaho	

Thanks also to Paul Fleischmann who contributed chapters 10 and 11; Jim Burns who contributed 12 and 13; and Bo Boshears whose many contributions appear throughout this book.

HOW TO MAX OUT THIS BOOK

Designing outreach events that actually reach lost kids takes mega effort. *The Magnet Effect* gives you a passion, a strategy and a step-by-step plan. It helps you to know where the outreach event fits in your ministry and then shows you how to break it down into "bite-sized chunks." With this book you can do outreach events without burning out. In fact, when you use the approach in this book eventually you will have so many people involved it will take less effort on your part! Not a bad deal!

So how do you get the most of what is in here?

First, read all of Part 1 and Part 2. That will give you the big picture.

Second, watch *The Magnet Effect Video*. This video will *show* you what an outreach event can look like. Since a picture is worth a thousand words, the video will give you a visual picture of excellence in creating an outreach event.

Third, work through "The Outreach Event Planner." Work on each aspect of it until you get that part completed. Then go on to the next part. <u>Do not skip over one part to get to another</u>. If you have not done each aspect then you will have a crack in your building that will eventually cause it to collapse. As you read through it you will think: "This will take me forever." Well, it won't take quite that long. But as the old saying goes: "If it's worth doing, it's worth doing right."

Fourth, in the process of implementing the first three, discover how you can network with other youth leaders in your area. This moves you beyond your local church, builds a web of positive, supportive relationships, and puts you in a position to influence your entire community or city. As a network you can do outreach events together that you could never do alone.

As you work through this process and it is moving slower than you think it should, remembering your ultimate objective will keep you going: **to reach every kid on every campus in your community.**

THE MAGNET EFFECT VIDEO

You can attract non-Christian students to hear the Gospel!
***The Magnet Effect Video* will show you how!**

Probably the greatest challenge to the church today is to reach beyond its four walls to challenge the younger generation to follow Jesus Christ. *The Magnet Effect Video* presents an "on the edge" approach to designing outreach events that draw kids to Christ.

In *The Magnet Effect Video* experienced youth leaders Barry St. Clair and Bo Boshers walk through an actual outreach event and then show how to put one together. They demonstrate the powerful impact an outreach event can have on a student's life. Then they display each element of a cutting edge outreach event as it is taking place. After the event is a presentation of a planning meeting that gives a step-by-step plan for putting an outreach event together.

The video is designed as a companion to *The Magnet Effect* book. In the video youth workers *see* what an effective outreach event looks like. In the book you *learn* the step-by-step process of putting one together. Both help youth leaders understand the strategy behind an outreach event and how to mobilize leaders and students to reach kids without Christ.

HOW TO DESIGN THE MAGNET EFFECT

One

Hit the Bull's-Eye: Targeting Kids

Ricky, his brother, and his sister each have different last names. His mom got pregnant with his older brother when she was a teenager. The guy never stayed around, so no one knew him. Then his mom had Ricky. He, too, was born out of wedlock. Ricky's father stayed with his family a couple of years, but it didn't work out. Later on Ricky's mom married a man who abused her. She endured that for a year before she left. Now Ricky is a senior in high school and the only child left at home. His mom has a new husband, the fourth man in her life. His brother and sister refuse to speak to Ricky because he refuses to get close to his stepfather. His comment: "You know, after having so many dads, it's hard to get close to one more."

Hurt. Disappointed. Stressed. Depressed. Dysfunctional. Angry. Frustrated. Bitter. Insecure. Sexually active. Rebellious. Undisciplined. Uncommitted. Drinking heavily. Pressured. Distrusting. Suicidal. Kids are experiencing incredible pain today. Outwardly they appear normal—friendly, open, cool, eager, funny, energetic. But just below the surface they desperately struggle with themselves and with their relationships.

You, as a youth leader, can connect names and faces to kids who fit these descriptions.

A whole generation of kids desperately needs the touch of Jesus Christ. The only way that will ever happen is for a whole army of people who have had a life-changing encounter with Jesus Christ to see teenagers the way God sees them, and to seek teenagers the way God seeks them.

SEE KIDS THE WAY GOD SEES THEM

Traveling in Romania with a group of 23 high school students can get a little ragged at times. On planes. Off planes. On buses. Off buses. On trains. Off trains. That's where it gets hairy. Usually the train stops for two to three minutes. All kids and all luggage need to get on or off quickly, very quickly. On more than one occasion I got on the train, which was already moving down the tracks, and wondered: "Did we get everybody and everything?" It's that *Home Alone* feeling: "Kevin!!!!!"

On a trip like that, one bag inevitably has essentials, such as passport, visa, money, message notes—irreplaceable stuff. This particular night we had all gotten on the train in the dark and in a big hurry. Somebody else put my bags on. After all the bodies settled, I began to look for my briefcase with the essentials. Nope. Not in this berth. Must be in the next one. Not in this berth either. "Has anybody seen my tan briefcase?" Now I was scrambling, searching, frantically asking, "Where's the tan briefcase?" I looked everywhere. No briefcase. IT WAS LOST!

My panicked tone of voice moved all 23 students into action, looking for the briefcase. My mind raced: *What if it was left on the track. I'll never see it again. You can get lots of money for an American passport.* Now I was pacing, wringing my hands, and feeling nauseated just thinking about it. *No passport or visa, I may never see my family again. All that money ... My message notes, years of work down the drain. I can never replace it. And it's* **lost***!* I yell out: "Look again! We're not going to rest until we find that briefcase!"

Those same feelings and thoughts must have been only a fraction of the concern Jesus had when He passed by that day and called Zacchaeus down immediately from the tree and gave him the gift of salvation. Jesus' entire purpose for coming as the Son of Man was "to seek and save that which was lost" (Luke 19:10).

God looks at today's generation of kids and sees almost all of them like Zacchaeus—LOST! He is still on a search-and-redeem mission. God's desire for us is that we would see kids the way He sees them—lost.

Unlike my search for my briefcase, from God's perspective lost doesn't have to do with distance, but with relationship. He went into great detail to help us get His point. Jesus told a series of three parables which actually become one story masterfully woven together to describe the nature of a person who is outside of Him. Certainly Luke 15 describes the present "lost generation" of young people.

Looking down the corridors of time at members of today's youth generation, Jesus pictures them as **lost sheep.** A sheep puts his face down in the green grass and begins to nibble. Enjoying the green grass in front of him, he wanders around doing what satisfies him at the moment. He has no sense of long-term purpose. A dog, a cat, a horse, a cow will all come back. Not a sheep. He keeps on nibbling until he nibbles himself over the side of a cliff, or becomes a "cast" sheep.

Philip Keller, in *A Shepherd Looks at the 23rd Psalm*, describes a cast sheep. If a sheep loses its balance it rolls over on its back and cannot get up. The sheep paws the air frantically to get back up, but it cannot do so. Gases build up inside its body. Circulation is cut off from the legs and, unless the sheep is rescued, it dies.[1]

So Jesus sees this generation of young people as sheep who have "gone astray and turned everyone to his own way" (Isaiah 53:6). Nibbling only at the pleasure in front of them, with no sense of purpose, they wander farther and farther away. On the edge of the cliff and off balance, teenagers today are in grave danger.

Looking at this generation, Jesus also describes it as a **lost coin.** A coin is not supposed to get lost, but is to be invested or spent. Its purpose is to turn a profit. But when it is lost, it is "unprofitable." That's how the Apostle Paul describes a person outside of Jesus Christ: All have turned away, and together they have become worthless (Rom. 3:12).

Like the woman searching for the coin, Jesus holds this generation in high value. God created today's teenagers to be invested, spent. He wants to put them to use. But because they are outside of Christ they have lost their usefulness. Why did the woman light a candle? Because the coin was lost in a dark place. Why did she sweep the floor? Because the coin was lost in the dirt. Kids in this generation have lost their usefulness in the darkness and dirtiness around them.[2]

Then Jesus describes the current youth generation as a **lost son.** The Prodigal Son wanted to spend his inheritance now. He got what he wanted and split. At first he lived "high on the hog." But when he had squandered his inheritance, he fed the pigs. He was desperate, depressed—in the pits. He set out to "get it all" but lost everything. What a vivid picture of this generation.

LOST. Yep. We all agree. The vast majority of this generation is lost. But, on an individual basis, what does that mean? Just as Jesus picked out Zacchaeus as an individual, He sees each one in the younger generation individually. And each one is lost individually. But what does a teenager look like who is lost? Can we get a composite that will help us understand more clearly how God sees each one, and how we need to see each one?

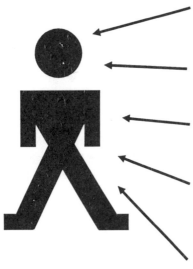

MENTAL—Experiences low self-esteem and boredom with life, resulting in depression.

EMOTIONAL—Feels aching loneliness and distrusts love, leading to stress.

PHYSICAL—Lacks self-control, resulting in poor habits such as abuse of alcohol, sex, and drugs.

SOCIAL—Interested in relationships, desperately wanting acceptance and performing to please peers; but short-circuits them by putting self first.

SPIRITUAL—Crippled by guilt and fear of death, leading to hopelessness.

As a result of these debilitating problems in their lives, a "philosophy of life" has developed that most North American students follow.

- *There is no right and wrong.* Kids have no absolutes, only opinions and circumstances. They are their own value system. What they think and believe is the ultimate authority.

- *If it feels good, do it.* The value used to be: "If it feels good, do it; as long as no one gets hurt." Now that value has been twisted into "If it feels good, do it; who cares who gets hurt."

- *The mind does not matter.* Due to the influence of MTV, CD's, and television, *entertainment* is more important than *education*. The continual drop in SAT scores underlines this.

- *Relationships are important if they help me.* And it follows then that "If they do not help me, I get out." They have learned this from their parents who are divorced and from living in a "throw away" environment.

- *I'm my own boss.* Authority makes no sense. Some young people actively rebel against it. Others just don't pay any attention to it. What parents, teachers and police say has no bearing because peer authority reigns. "I make my own rules."

- *I'm living for today.* Because they know they can't "have it all" like their parents did, they feel a hopelessness about the future. Having lost their dream of "personal peace and affluence," they try to enjoy life today with no thought for tomorrow.

From this composite we can see why kids have such serious problems individually. When we multiply this to every kid in every school in the nation, it becomes clear that we have a mess on our hands. What are some of the underlying issues that are aggravating their problems?

The Apostle Paul got to the heart of it when he exclaimed, "We have worshipped and served the creature rather than the Creator" (Rom. 1:25). In Romans 1 the apostle goes on to explain what happens as a result of that root problem.

Education without Truth. Paul says that "wicked men suppress the truth [v. 18] ... their thinking became futile [v. 21] ... although they claimed to be wise they became fools [v. 22]." Because the environment that our kids live in every day has forsaken the search for the truth, anarchy reigns in our school systems. In jest students used to sing the old grade-school song:

> We have gathered here together for the burning of the school.
> We have tortured every teacher, we have broken every rule.
> We have set the school on fire, we have killed the principal.
> Our truth is marching on.

That song is a joke no longer! The National Institute of Education estimates monthly

- 5,200 junior and senior high teachers are attacked.
- 6,000 students are robbed by force.
- 282,000 are assaulted.
- 112,000 robberies occur.[3]

A generation ago the top offenses in the public schools were:

- Talking
- Chewing gum
- Making noise
- Running in the halls
- Getting out of turn in line
- Wearing improper clothing
- Not putting paper in wastebaskets

Today the top public school offenses are:

1. Rape
2. Robbery
3. Assault
4. Burglary
5. Arson
6. Bombings
7. Murder
8. Suicide
9. Absenteeism
10. Vandalism
11. Extortion
12. Drug abuse
13. Alcohol abuse
14. Gang warfare
15. Pregnancies
16. Abortions
17. Venereal disease[4]

As a result education has been totally disrupted.

In a recent survey of 8,000 high school juniors conducted by the National Endowment for the Humanities:

- Only half knew which half century the Civil War or World War I was fought.
- One third of the students placed the arrival of Columbus in the New World after 1750.
- Only one third knew Geoffery Chaucer as the author of *The Canterbury Tales.*[5]

Another survey, called the National Assessment of Educational Progress, showed that only half of 17-year-olds have the capacity to write and to organize their ideas on paper.

According to the Hudson Institute, achievement scores are down over the last ten years due to "permissiveness, promiscuity, violence and crime."[6]

Sex without Purity. Very logically the Apostle Paul shows us the results of lostness when he says, "Therefore God gave them over in the sinful desires of their hearts to sexual impurity...shameful lusts ...women (and men) exchanged natural relations for unnatural ones ...and received the due penalty for their perversion" (Rom. 1:24-27).

In our sex-crazed society the natural result is that kids are participating in sex at younger and younger ages. The National Center for Health Statistics reports that 29 percent of 15-year-old girls are sexually active, as are 81 percent of 19-year-olds! Boys are no less active. Seventy-two percent of 17-year-old boys and 88 percent of 19-year-olds are sexually active.

The consequences of that are appalling. Every year 1.5 million abortions are occurring. Thirty-eight sexually transmitted diseases have reached epidemic proportions. In three years the number of cases of syphillis has risen 62 percent[7]. That is not to mention the spread of AIDS. One of every 250 men in America is now HIV positive. And one out of every six college girls gets raped. So the story continues...

Society without God. Our society and its effect on the younger generation line up pretty well with what the Apostle Paul wrote in Romans 1: "He gave them over...to what ought not to be done. They have become filled with every kind of wickedness, evil, greed and depravity" (1:28-29).

A society that fits this description has produced the present generation of kids. Four primary forces shape their lives. One is their peers, which we will not discuss here. We can see here what a dominant effect the other three have.

Parents. With well over half the teenagers living in single parent homes, and over 65 percent of all mothers working outside the home, it is little wonder that parents don't spend time with their kids. According to George Barna, among teens whose father is present in the home, the average amount of time discussing things that matter is less than 40 minutes per week. (Ten percent say they spend no time at all in such discussions.) In homes where the mother is present, the amount of time spent with her discussing matters of interest to the teen averages 55 minutes per week.[8] Only 52 percent of 15- to 18-year-olds say they are satisfied with their current family situation.[9]

William Bennett, former Secretary of Education, summarized the situation this way:

> Where are the fathers?...Generally, the mothers are there strug-
> gling. For nine out of ten children in single parent homes, the
> father is the one who isn't there. One-fifth of all American chil-
> dren live in homes without fathers....Where are the fathers?
> Where are the men? Wherever they are, this much is clear: too
> many are not with their children.[10]

It doesn't take long for kids to realize "If I'm going to survive, I had better look out for me."

Television. At high school graduation young people have watched 15,000 hours of television. That is 3,000 more hours than they have spent in the classroom. With the exception of sleep, youth spend more time watching TV than in any other activity. They will have seen:

- 350,000 commercials

- 18,000 murders

- Over 20,000 instances of sexual intercourse or foreplay

- Drinking by their favorite characters over 50 times a week.

The American Academy of Pediatrics recently urged that children should not watch TV more than two hours a day in order to limit the damage caused by violence and sexual programming.[11] No wonder such heavy exposure to TV sex and violence results in kids imitating those same acts in real life.

Rock Music. A subcommittee of the American Medical Association reports that the average teenager listens to 10,500 hours of rock music between the seventh and twelfth grades.[12] Evidence is rampant that certain types of music contribute to emotional dysfunction in kids, including drug abuse, premarital sex, and violence. As I write I'm staring at a recent *Newsweek* cover entitled "When Is Rap 2 Violent?" Featuring Snoop Doggy Dogg, the cover comments: "His album hits the top of the charts this week. Last week, he was indicted for murder."

It's not hard to figure out why kids are killing each other, and why others are frightened to walk down the hall at school or go into the restroom.

EVERY 24 HOURS
in America this is what happens to teenagers:

2,989	children see their parents get divorced.
2,556	children are born out of wedlock.
1,629	children are in adult jails.
3,288	children run away from home.
1,849	children are abused or neglected.
1,512	teenagers drop out of school.
437	children are arrested for drinking or drunken driving.
211	children are arrested for drug abuse.
2,795	teens (women under 20) get pregnant.
7,742	teenagers become sexually active.
1,106	teenagers have abortions.
1,295	teenagers give birth.
372	teenagers miscarry.
623	teenagers contract syphilis or gonorrhea.
6	teenagers commit suicide.

(Source: Children's Defense Fund; Jan. 8, 1990)

Without much effort we could get depressed over this scene. But a more proper response is to get our heads out of the sand, see the situation in our society as it really is, understand the intense pressure kids face as a result, know from the bibical perspective that they do not have the internal resources to handle it because they are lost, and then take the challenge to help "find" them through introducing them to Jesus Christ.

We can do all this with great confidence because, in spite of all the complications in kid's lives, Jesus really is the only answer. Pascal, the great French scientist and philosopher, was correct when he said: "There is a God-shaped vacuum in the heart of every man that cannot be filled by any created thing, but only by God, the Creator, made known through Jesus Christ."

As we see teenagers the way God sees them—lost, with all of its accompanying pain and hurt—He will give us a deep desire to seek them the way He seeks them, so they can be found!

SEEK KIDS THE WAY GOD SEEKS THEM

On that train in Romania, frantically searching for my valuable briefcase, all of us tore up the place to see if we could find it. We were intense, focused. We had our "game faces" on. We organized into teams, each team taking a berth. All of us, at the same time, were focused on the same objective—find the briefcase.

And we did! It had been placed behind two or three other boxes and suitcases. When we found it we shouted, then we laughed. I let out a big sigh of relief. I was excited to have it back. Finding that briefcase made my day.

Those same kinds of emotions must have flooded over Jesus when Zacchaeus came down from that tree. The Bible says that Zacchaeus received Jesus "joyfully." Certainly they rejoiced together when Jesus said, "Today salvation has come to this house" (Luke 19:9).

When something or someone is lost, we see a pattern:

Intense concentration ⇒ Joyful celebration.

Isn't that true with the lost sheep, the lost coin, and the lost son? After the intense concentration to find what was lost, Jesus says, "there is rejoicing in the presence of the angels of God over one sinner who repents" (Luke 15:10).

Finding what is lost is God's nature. Adrian Rogers put it this way:

> When we see Jesus going out after the sheep, we see the rescuing nature of Jesus. When we see the woman with the lost coin we see the revealing nature of the Holy Spirit. When we see the father welcoming the son back, we see the receiving nature of God the Father.[13]

When we have had our lives radically changed by the seeking Savior, then we too have built into our new nature that same desire to see people who are lost become found.

What distinguishes one youth leader from another? Both have the same gifts and abilities, both have the same human resources, but one attracts kids like crazy and the other one does not. What is the difference?

A **burden** for those who are lost.

With the following graphic story Dick Hillis illustrates where most of us are.

> As I watched the evening news, a young man named Cecil walked into the picture. Suddenly, he sat down on the curb in front of the whirling camera and set himself aflame. When the pain became more than he could bear, he jumped to his feet and raced down the street. Before the camera turned away, all one could see was Cecil totally engulfed by the flames. I sat there stunned. Then the question! Were the cameramen more interested in taking a picture than in saving Cecil from the horror of being burned alive?[14]

That story nails most of us! Indifference indicts us. How strangely different Jesus' burden is from that of many twentieth-century youth leaders.

- "He had **compassion** on them, because they were harassed and helpless" (Matt. 9:36).

- "Jesus **wept"** (John 11:35).

- Jesus was "**deeply moved** in spirit and **troubled**" because of the death of Lazarus (John 11:33).

- Jesus cried out: "O Jerusalem, Jerusalem . . . how often I have **longed** to gather your children together" (Luke 13:34).

Not allowing the love of the Spirit of Jesus to flow through us, we express apathy about Christ and about people. Therefore we come across to the lost in a way that causes them not to want to be found! We exhibit one or all of the qualities of Galatians 5:19-21. But when we are empowered by the love of the Spirit, we are charged with enthusiasm about Christ and we find ways to love other people. Therefore we become attractive to lost people who, then, want to be found. When we are empowered by the Spirit we exhibit the qualities of Galatians 5:22-23.

Dr. William Abraham focuses the issue for us in his remarkable statement:

> We live in a world where people are addicted to drugs, to greed, to racism, to terrorism and to a host of sins that will not be tackled without the fullness of the reign of God in our midst...What is needed is not just more talk, or more programs ...but the mysterious power of the Holy Spirit...

As we allow the Holy Spirit to empower us He will release in us the love and compassion that will give us that burden for kids. Then we can pray this profound prayer: LORD, BREAK MY HEART WITH THE THINGS THAT BREAK THE HEART OF GOD.

I experienced the reality of that prayer recently. Having completed my message to a group of 600 high school students over one Christmas, I watched them as they responded. It was beautiful to see all those potential-laden lives so eager to please God. I was ready to sit down when suddenly, seemingly out of nowhere, emotion overwhelmed me. I began to weep in front of those kids. It took several moments to bring myself under control. Through tears these words came out: "I want to ask you to forgive me and my generation for leaving you the lousiest legacy in American history. Your generation has some severe problems because of what we have done to you. But I want you to know that I, for one, have committed my life to see that you become whole again. I believe that God not only wants to restore you but also to release you to become the generation that finishes taking the message of Christ to the ends of the earth—that fulfills the Great Commission."

None of that was planned or contrived. Simply, God was breaking my heart with the things that break His heart. I realized I had a burden for those kids and the generation they represent. God's desire is that we see kids the way He sees them, and that we then seek them the way He seeks them. When we do, they will become our target and we will become their magnet that draws them to Christ.

ACTION POINT

1. Spend an hour alone with God this week asking Him to help you see kids—particularly lost kids—the way He sees them. Write down what He shows you.

_____

_____

_____

2. Spend another hour with God asking Him to break your heart for kids—or continue doing so—in a way that will cause you to seek kids the way He wants to seek them. Write down what He tells you to do.

_____

_____

_____

1. Philip Keller, *A Shepherd Looks at the 23rd Psalm* (Grand Rapids: Zondervan, 1978), 61.

2. Adapted from an article by Adrian Rogers in *Decision* magazine, March 1982.

3. National Institute of Education, as quoted in *Youthletter*, Evangelical Ministries, Inc. Philadelphia, Pa.

4. *USA Today*, September 10, 1985.

5. *New York Times*, September 8, 1992. Cited in Youth Worker Update, November 1992.

6. Quoted in *Youthletter*, Evangelical Ministries, Inc. Philadelphia, Pa.

7. James Dobson and Gary Bauer, *Children at Risk* (Waco, Tex.: Word, 1992), 9-10.

8. George Barna,"Today's Teens: A Generation in Transition," newsletter, 10.

9. *Ibid.*, 9.

10. William J. Bennett, *Our Children and Our Country* (New York: Simon & Schuster, 1988), 64.

11. *USA Today*, April 17, 1990, Dobson and Bauer, *Children at Risk*, 207.

12. "Love of Heavy Rock May Be Tied to Teen Drugs, Sex," AMA Neuhaus News Service, Sept. 22,1989; Dobson and Bauer, *Children at Risk*, 213.

13. Adrian Rogers, "Hope for Lost Mankind," *Decision*, March 1982.

14. Dick Hillis, *Lost and Found* 5:1 (Spring 1986).

Two

Look Right Here: Focusing on Fruit

"Mike, a high school senior, visited our mid-week youth outreach event for the first time a year ago."

That's how one youth pastor started the story. Then he told of an incredible chain of events that have taken place since then. He said that Mike came to the outreach event because Ricardo, a young man the youth pastor was discipling, invited him. After Mike attended for three weeks, Ricardo led him to Christ and into the church. Shortly after that, Mike began to reach out to his friends with the gospel. He eagerly attended an evangelism seminar and learned more about how to share his faith.

Mike's fresh, new faith and radical lifestyle change got the attention of his parents and older brother. None of them attended church nor were they professing Christians. Within a short period of time all three of them received Christ and now actively serve the Lord in church. Mike's parents have recently volunteered to become youth sponsors in the ministry and his brother has gotten involved in a ministry group on his college campus.

This summer Mike reached out to a good friend named Greg. He brought Greg to the same outreach event where he met Christ. Greg received Christ. He then led his two friends, Kelly and Ken, to Christ. Greg, Kelly and Ken have recently reached out to two other guys, inviting them to the outreach event. Now all five of them have formed a ministry team that comes early every week to set up for the outreach event. In one year this exciting process has resulted in seven significant, long-lasting conversions.[1]

Probably nothing gets talked about more, but gets done less, than genuine, life-changing evangelism. We expend incredible amounts of energy on rallies, crusades, tours, concerts, church-league softball (or a myriad of other sports), trips, camps, retreats, skiing, and on we go, ad infinitum, ad nauseum. But how many young people actually hear, understand, and respond to the message of the gospel? How many have a genuine, life-changing experience with Jesus through these events and are living for Him three weeks afterward?

One youth pastor expressed his frustration over spinning his wheels:

> For years I busied myself with "the good things" of youth minis-
> try instead of slowing down to face the reality that my ministry
> was almost ignoring "the best thing" that Christ called us to do
> ...that thing is life-changing evangelism. It was after coming
> face to face with the reality that I was working myself to
> death, yet failing to change the lives of youth for eternity, that
> I began to get serious about the role of life-changing evangelism
> in youth ministry.

So how can we change the focus of our events to genuine evangelism?

FOCUSING ON FRUIT

Rather than focusing on the number of students who attend the event, or the number who accept Jesus Christ, as important as those might be, the outreach event is designed to accomplish two objectives. First, produce *life change* in the lives of the young people who attend. In other words, we genuinely desire that they have a serious encounter with Jesus Christ. Secondly, help students—those who were already Christians and the ones who newly meet Christ—to become *life changers*. After they encounter Christ, they take the challenge to influence their peers for Jesus Christ.

Changing lives goes far beyond an initial response at an event. It centers in on the complete reconstruction of the person. As we think about the focus of an outreach event, it must be that teenagers experience salvation—the kind Jesus describes in John 15:16, "You did not choose me, but I chose you to go and bear fruit—fruit that will last."

We're not talking about racking up decisions, filling out cards, or joining anything. We are talking about helping kids encounter Jesus in such a way that every aspect of their lives is captured by Christ.

As Jesus expounds on "fruit bearing," He tells us what brings about such an encounter. He expresses a good word to us in youth ministry about how our events should touch kids' lives in a fruit-bearing way.

Connection with the vine. Jesus said, "I am the vine: you are the branches" (John 15:5). As we think about putting together events, this relational reality moves us quickly away from desiring any superficial response from kids and toward helping them come into a vital union with the Vine. That doesn't preclude fun and crazy stuff, but it does mean we know what we want to happen to kids.

Cutting away the worthless branches. Jesus said, "He cuts off every branch in me that bears no fruit, while every branch that does bear fruit he trims clean so it will be even more fruitful" (John 15:2). Jesus wants to cut out of students' lives anything that will hinder them from producing fruit. Kids will come to our outreach events with some pretty severe struggles, ideas far from the truth, and way-out lifestyles. As we address their needs, struggles, and issues, and as they see Jesus as the Need Meeter, they will rid themselves of their old lifestyles that "bear no fruit" and become grafted into Christ, who will conform them to His image and make them "even more fruitful." We need to have a youth ministry generally and outreach events specifically prepared to operate as "hedge trimmers" in kids' lives.

Control of the fruitful branches. Jesus said, "Remain in me, and I will remain in you. No branch can bear fruit by itself; it must remain in the vine. Neither can you bear fruit unless you remain in me" (John 15:4). "Remain" means to stay put. Once a teenager responds at an outreach event he must have the kind of personal help that will help him to "stay put" in his walk with Christ as he faces life's pain and pressures. Only in a youth ministry environment of nourishment, encouragement, and accountability will he be able to "remain."

Focusing on "fruitbearing" will help us produce the kind of excellent event that helps kids change and gives them the opportunity to pass that change on to their friends. This kind of focus will move individual students as well as the entire youth ministry through the progression that Jesus outlines in John 15:

- "No fruit" (v.2)
  - "Fruit" (v. 3)
    - "Much fruit" (v. 5)
      - "Fruit that will last" (v. 16)

The focus of the outreach event is to present Jesus Christ in such a way that they will *change*—from "no fruit" to "fruit that will last." Fruitful attitudes, actions, habits, and lifestyles will produce Christian kids with a credibility that will cause non-Christian kids to respect them for the *life change* they have experienced and listen to their message.

Without this kind of focus you will work with uncommitted or half-committed students who will drain your time, undermine any credibility your youth group has with non-Christians, leave you as the Lone Ranger to pull off a highly labor-intensive event, and create an atmosphere that resembles a funeral.

Let's put this in perspective. Would you rather have 1,000 cars that take you 100 miles each, or one car that will take you 100,000 miles? What a hassle if you had to change cars every 100 miles—walking back to get the other car. You wouldn't get anywhere. If you "buy" the right focus from the beginning, then you won't have continual "breakdowns." Nothing short of fruitful, changed lives will get the job done. Even though you will want as many students at the outreach event as possible, the focus is on fruit.

PROGRAMMING WITH PURPOSE

If our focus is fruit—encouraging life change and producing life changers—then we need to *program with purpose.* In order to have programs with a fruitbearing purpose, it stands to reason that we need to know what the specific purpose of the event is.

Until we see God's purpose, we will struggle with our motivation in putting on events for kids. And certainly an inadequate perspective will carry over to our volunteers and our youth group as well.

So many youth leaders complain to me about the apathy of their students and volunteer leaders.

- "Too busy."
- "They only come because their parents make them."
- "Kids are apathetic because their parents don't care."
- "All they do is goof off."
- "They complain, 'This is boring. When are we going to do something fun?'"
- "They aren't interested because we can't entertain them like the world entertains them."

So kids drop in if it suits them, or they don't if that suits them better. They have no real excitement about the youth group. When they do come it's like they have parked their bodies at the meeting but their minds are somewhere else. They keep asking, "When is this going to be over?" So you keep on trying to think up bigger and better gimmicks, games and group trips in order to keep them entertained. The group slowly shrinks in size because few new students come and others drop out.

Is it possible to motivate those same apathetic students and then challenge them to bring their friends at school to hear about Jesus Christ? The answer is yes, *if*

- you have a compelling burden for lost kids (chapter 1)
- you have an overall strategy for your youth ministry (chapter 3)
- you have the purpose for your event clearly in mind (this chapter).

You've begun the process of developing a compelling burden for lost students, now let's deal with getting your event purpose clearly in mind.

Any time we put on an outreach event for young people the following overarching purpose should drive everything we do:

To present the life-changing message of Christ

In a culturally relevant manner

To lost young people.

To present the life-changing message of Christ. Your outreach events exist for the purpose of communicating the claims of Christ clearly. It sounds simple enough but it's not as easy as it sounds. Several challenges stand in our way.

Knowing the message. If the life, death, resurrection of Jesus, and release of the Spirit to change lives is fuzzy to us, then certainly it will be fuzzy to our kids.

Preparing the message. "Chasing around like a wild man (woman)" because your priorities are out of order squeezes out time for preparing a clear message.

Communicating the message. Even if we know the message and have prepared it, one of the hardest tasks in the world is taking what would be clear in the adult world and bringing it to the level that kids can grasp. As somebody once said, "We need to get the cookies on the lower shelf so the kids can reach them."

The Master Teacher tells us how to present the claims about Himself. We see how He did it from the example in John 7:37-39, "On the last and greatest day of the Feast, Jesus stood and said in a loud voice, 'If anyone is thirsty, let him come to me and drink. Whoever believes in me, as the Scripture has said, streams of living water will flow from within him.'"

In the midst of a large crowd at the Feast of Booths in Jerusalem, Jesus proclaimed who He was to the crowd. He presented Himself clearly so that people could understand and respond.

The Feast of Booths was a ceremonial reminder that the children of Israel had been wanderers in the desert where water was precious and difficult to find. During the ceremony a priest took a golden pitcher, walked down to the Pool of Siloam, and filled it with water. He carried the water back through a special gate used just for this ceremony—the Water Gate—while the people recited Isaiah 12:3, "With joy will you draw water from the wells of salvation." He carried the water to the temple and poured it on the altar as an offering to God.

The whole ceremony dramatized thanksgiving for God's good gift of water, a prayer for rain, and a remembrance of the water which sprang from the rock when Moses struck it with his staff. During this ceremony, perhaps at that very moment, Jesus' words rang out: "If a man is thirsty, let him come to Me and drink."[2]

Jesus spoke clearly in a language that every person there understood. No one missed the message that He was that Living Water symbolized in that ceremony. On this hot and dusty day He invited them to come and have their needs met—have a drink. Then He made a promise that whoever believed would have rivers of Living Water flowing through him! WOW!

The challenge for us is to present the claims of Christ in such a compelling way that young people will understand who Jesus is and will want to drink. We want to make our outreach event such a magnet event that kids can't but be drawn to the Living Water.

In a culturally relevant manner. Your outreach event is not for the pastor, deacons, elders, or parents. If it were designed for them then we wouldn't do some of the "wild and crazy" things we do. This is a meeting for kids.

Therefore, *Christian kids need to feel comfortable bringing their friends.* If a student thinks that what happens at these meetings is "dorky," then you can know that he will not bring anyone whom he likes to this meeting. He might bring a kid he wants to mug afterward. For that reason, creating a positive atmosphere is crucial. Let's look at what Levi did in Luke 5:27-32 to see a great model on how to do that.

First, we see that Levi had just met Christ himself: "After this, Jesus went out and saw a tax collector by the name of Levi sitting at his tax booth. 'Follow me,' Jesus said to him, and Levi got up, left everything and followed him" (vv. 27-28).

The best and biggest path back to the world of lost kids is young people who have just recently come from that world. When a kid has "left everything and followed him" he or she will have a deep desire for friends to do the same.

Second, Levi, now a believer, wanted his friends to know Jesus, "Then Levi held a great banquet for Jesus at his house, and a large crowd of tax collectors and others [sinners] were eating with them" (v. 29). Levi had a party! He designed this party to share the new life he had found.

Fun is a value held in high esteem by kids. Yet most students, when asked what it means to be a Christian, will tell you something like this: "Following a bunch of rules." "Going to church." "Doing good things and not doing bad things." That is why it is so important to present Jesus in a context that is not dull and boring. When we put together a magnet event, kids need to walk away saying, "Wow, that was great. That was sooooo much fun!" We can communicate that "Hanging around Jesus is the greatest fun you will ever have."

Finally, notice that Levi set an atmosphere where he felt comfortable having Jesus around his friends and his friends around Jesus. Christian students need to feel comfortable bringing their friends to these events. That will hinge on whether or not we can create a magnetic atmosphere where warmth, acceptance, and love will draw kids to Jesus Christ.

And non-Christian kids need to feel comfortable coming. To make non-Christian kids feel comfortable we need *to create an environment with high energy enthusiasm.* Levi's banquet wasn't just your normal banquet—it was a *"great* banquet." And it wasn't just a little group of friends, it was a *large* crowd. Imagine the energy in that room.

The very word *enthusiasm* means "in God." It seems only natural to have a bundle of enthusiasm at a Christian meeting, especially with kids. The MTV generation feels very comfortable in that kind of large, loud event. That sense of enthusiasm arouses the interest of lost kids, just like it did on another day, at another time, when Jesus taught by the lake: "The crowd that gathered around him was so large that he got into a boat and sat in it out on the lake, while all the people were along the shore at the water's edge" (Mark 4:1).

The enthusiasm of the people expressed itself at such a high level that they almost pushed Jesus into the water. I've always seen this as one of the humorous incidents in the Gospels. The more Jesus taught, healed, and delivered people from the demonic, the more excited they became. As they crowded in on Him, He had to backpedal. Soon He was at the edge of the water and had no place else to go. One more step and He would have been soaked. Either someone saw the situation and brought a boat, or one was already there. At just the last minute Jesus deftly made His move into the boat, avoiding a dunking.

Your outreach events can create that same kind of enthusiatic excitement.

Also, to help non-Christian kids feel comfortable we need to *take the gospel to the streets*. Notice that Jesus took his message outside the four walls of the church (the synagogue) into a home and by a lake among crowds of ordinary men and women.

Many youth workers struggle with this because they have ministered only within the four walls of the church, a setting which is comfortable and familiar.

I grew up in the church. The only Christian events I had ever seen were inside the church. So one of the greatest opportunities I have ever had to sharpen my youth ministry skills came when I was in college. I led a "club" every week that met in the living room of someone's home. Kids, mostly non-Christians, came—ones that others and I had built relationships with at the school. Every week was wild. I didn't always relate well. I had a lot to learn. But in this "baptism by fire" I discovered how to present Christ outside the religious confines of the church. Just the other day I saw a youth minister who reminded me that he came to Christ in one of those meetings.

Later I discovered I was in good company with my struggle. John Wesley had a difficult time moving outside the church setting. He was a faithful servant of the Church of England. West of London, in Bristol, his friend George Whitefield was preaching to the miners. As many as 20,000 at a time listened in the open air. His hearers were coming to Christ by the hundreds, so he sent for John Wesley and asked him to preach outdoors.

Wesley hesitated. He wrote, "I love a commodious room, a soft cushion, a handsome pulpit." Open-air preaching offended him. He said, "I could scarcely reconcile myself at first to this strange way—having been all my life (till very lately) so tenacious of every point relating to decency and order, that I should have thought the saving of souls almost a sin if it had not been done in a church." But Wesley realized that outdoor preaching brought people to Jesus. He said, "I cannot argue against a matter of fact."[3] And, as they say, the rest is history.

The only "culturally relevant manner" most lost kids will relate to will be what we do outside the confines of the church. But practically speaking, we may not be able to have some of our outreach events outside the four walls of the church. While it is best to have these events in a neutral, non-church setting, the option remains to have them inside your church building. If we are giving the non-Christian student the priority in our thinking and planning of the event, and if we are building relationships with them, meeting their needs, talking to them in their environment and inviting them to the event, whether the event is outside or inside the church building, then "if we build it, they will come."

To lost young people. This magnet event must welcome all students, regardless of culture, background, or level of commitment. For many in a traditional local church context this is a *huge* statement to make. Sometimes the church can be the biggest barrier that keeps people from Christ.

Jesus knew that better than anyone. It was the "religious establishment" (scribes, Pharisees, Sadducees, and the Sanhedrin) who resisted Jesus, even hated Him, and eventually killed Him. Now that is a sobering thought for some, because they know they have people in their churches who are just like that. Any time you even think about coloring outside the lines, you get your hand slapped. If kids come to your meeting who have purple hair, four earrings in each ear and one in each nostril, and who smoke and leave the butts in the parking lot, you know you are in trouble. I have no easy solutions for that one. But Jesus has been there before you, and He fought negative attitudes toward outsiders every step of the way.

You also have fine, well-meaning Christians who, like the disciples in Mark 10:13, want to protect Jesus and themselves from "sinful people." People were bringing little children to Jesus to have Him touch them, but the disciples rebuked them.

I have found that often parents and church people get all up in arms when "different" kids start hanging around. They want to protect their kids from these "evil influences," forgetting that their kids hang around these evil influences six to eight hours a day at school.

Steve, a seminary student at the time and now on our staff, was working on the staff of a church as a youth intern. He met some guys at school who hung out at a kids' night club. So he started going there to relate to those guys. They suggested that Steve start a Bible study on Monday nights at the night club. He did and lots of kids came. In a couple of months over thirty had accepted Christ. That's great. What was not so great was that when he brought those kids to church the parents got mad, the church kids rejected them, and the deacons voted that those young people could not come to the church any more.

That sad commentary is the result of actions by well-meaning Christian people (some of whom I know personally). Why did they do that? They had never thought through the implications of the Gospel, which says, "whosoever will may come."

Look at how Jesus handled the situation in Mark 10:

> When Jesus saw this, he was indignant. He said to them, "Let the little children come to me, and do not hinder them, for the kingdom of God belongs to such as these. I tell you the truth, anyone who will not receive the kingdom of God like a little child will never enter it." And He took the children in his arms, put his hands on them, and blessed them (Mark 10:14-16).

Jesus welcomed the children with open arms. This incident took place when Jesus was on His way to the Cross. The shadow of the Cross could never have been far from His mind, but He still took time for kids. He made time to take them in His arms, smile at them, and play with them for a while. The disciples wanted to keep them away from Jesus to protect Him and His precious time from people who were not important enough. But Jesus knew better. With the little time He had left, He still said, "Let the little children come to me."

Like the disciples did, it is easy to categorize groups of students as "not good enough." Because of their background, culture, color, age, attitudes, dress, and habits we fall into the trap of excluding people from the Gospel. Yet Jesus welcomes everyone. And as representatives of Jesus, as people who have His Spirit living in us, we must say along with Him: "Ya'll come!"

Here's the bottom line: with *focusing on fruit* and *programming with purpose* clearly established in your heart and mind, you can turn your weekly youth meeting, or any event for that matter, into a magnet that draws kids to Christ.

ACTION POINT

1. From what you have discovered in this chapter, write out a one-sentence purpose statement that clearly sets out your desire to focus on fruit and to program with purpose in any outreach events you do. Work on it at least 30 minutes every day this week.

_____

_____

_____

2. Go over your mission statement with at least two trusted friends to get their feedback. Then revise it on the basis of their input.

_____

_____

_____

_____

3. Prepare your mission statement for a later presentation to your pastor and your youth leaders. Type it up and put it on a large poster or overhead transparency.

_____

_____

_____

_____

1. This story is from Rick Caldwell, who over the years has had a phenomenal ministry of putting what's in this book into practice.
2. Adapted from William Barclay, _The Gospel of John_, vol. 1., rev. ed. The Daily Study Bible Series (Philadelphia: Westminster, 1975).
3. Adapted from William Barclay, _The Gospel of Mark_, rev. ed. The Daily Study Bible Series (Philadelphia: Westminster, 1975).

Three

Lay Tracks to Run On:
Setting Out a Strategy

As soon as I graduated from seminary, I was invited to become director of youth evangelism for my denomination. At 26 years of age I was very inexperienced in youth ministry. Although I had worked with kids for several years both in church and parachurch ministries, I had never *directed* anybody.

My first month on the job I came to the stark realization that I had no idea what to do. Not wanting to appear too stupid, I decided to take some survey trips to learn from what other people were doing. One of those trips took me to California. When I met with people there, one after the other asked me, "Have you talked to Chuck Miller?" "No, I've never heard of the guy." When his name kept coming up I decided to call him. He suggested that I meet him at 6:00 A.M. on Tuesday at a breakfast for kids. Sorry I asked! I tried to suggest another time, but he insisted. The real kicker was that we were on opposite sides of Los Angeles, which meant I had to get up at 4:00 A.M.

Do you ever get up in the morning and do "bedside battle"? The alarm goes off. Unconsciously you sit up on the side of the bed. In a stupor you begin to semi-reason with yourself: "I'm so tired. I have to drive in the smog. This bed feels sooo good. Only three snotty-nosed kids will show up for this. I love to sleep. This guy won't tell me anything new. This is a great pillow."

My sense of obligation finally got to me. I got up, drove across L.A., walked into the church. Three hundred kids were eating pancakes off paper plates! (We're talking big-time mess here.) I couldn't believe it. "They must have DC Talk coming in for a concert," I figured. Actually, they had no big production—a few songs, announcements, skit, a message, a response time. That's all. And off they went to school. *What's going on here?* I asked myself.

Later that morning Chuck and I ate breakfast (a real breakfast) at a little cafe and talked. He showed me how his highest priority was his own worship and walk with God. Then he described his leadership team of about 20 adults. After that he helped me see how those 20 adults disciple six to eight students each. From there he sketched out how each of those students has taken the responsibility to bring two or three of their friends each week. With each concept he pointed out how Jesus or Paul had followed the concept in the New Testament.

For the first time in my life I saw that *youth ministry is not an event but a process.* Instead of stringing a bunch of activities together and calling it a youth ministry, as I had done, I began to see that the real ministry takes place week to week in relationships. Instead of running myself ragged trying to get kids to come to an event, I could multiply myself through my leaders and discipled kids. For the first time it dawned on me: *This is God's strategy for fulfilling the Great Commission!*

In order for any outreach event, of any size, to be effective, it has to be built on the focus of the last chapter—*producing life change and life changers.* In light of that, then, you need to ask the serious question: "Is my ministry structured to produce life change and life changers?" For some this will require a major paradigm shift from *programs* to *relationships.* Your ministry needs a strategy designed to move leaders and students from one life-changing step to another. They need a track to run on.

FIVE ESSENTIALS OF EXCELLENT YOUTH MINISTRY

The New Testament lays out that track for us. In the process of the Christian life a person moves according to his or her own growth, from one phase to the next. The process may be represented as follows:

NON-BELIEVER → CONVERT → DISCIPLE → WORKER → LEADER

Goal:	Goal:	Goal:	Goal:	Goal:
Evangelize	Establish	Equip	Execute	Extend

I like to call the foregoing elements the *five essentials of excellent youth ministry*. *Essential* means non-negotiable, absolute, have to, no other way, got to do it, no way around it. My years of experience have shown me that you and I will never have an excellent youth ministry over the long haul unless all five of these essentials are evident in a finely-tuned balance.

For *the five essentials* to work for us, we need to lay them out into a workable strategy.

One of the tragic flaws in thinking about youth ministry is to believe that everyone in the group has to go and grow together—at the same time, at the same rate. Such a growth pattern has never happened before. It is not happening now. And it will never happen. That is because people are at all different stages in their thinking and in their growth. Because of that we need a strategy to help people grow whatever their level of maturity. For example:

- if a student is lost, the goal is to introduce him to Jesus Christ.

- if a student comes to Christ, the goal is to get him started in his walk with Christ.

- if a student starts growing, the goal is to help him move toward maturity and ministry.

- if a student matures, the goal is to make him a leader.

- if a new leader leads, the goal is to multiply his ministry through others.

What we have listed here is a "bottom up" approach. I would now like for us to look at the five essentials from a "top down" perspective, beginning with the leader.

LEADER

(Extending your ministry under the lordship of Christ)

LEADERSHIP TEAM

(Executing the ministry with volunteer workers)

DISCIPLES

(Equipping students to move toward maturity and ministry)

CONVERTS

(Establishing students in their faith)

NON-BELIEVERS

(Evangelizing lost kids)

Let's pause right here and make sure we're all on the same page. I am not offering you five easy steps to youth ministry success. How many times have you ordered a manual, kit, or something that came in a box that promised "7 Easy Steps to the Largest Youth Group in the Western Hemisphere"? Though slickly packaged and containing some elements of truth, more often than not the promises prove hollow. Like a $23 suit, the fit just isn't right for your situation.

Instead, my strategy has its roots firmly planted in the soil of the New Testament. Its base is the local church. And it is a strategy, not a program. A program has the same application in every situation. A strategy looks at needs, sets goals, and then makes application based on New Testament principles. That is why it works in large churches and small ones, in urban and suburban settings, and across cultures around the globe.

Before you jump into making a big splash with a series of big events, it is crucial that the five essentials operate with excellence in your ministry. Otherwise you will overextend yourself, doing yourself, your family, and your church more harm than good. Think of these five essentials as the best and fastest highway that will get you to your destination.

LIVING UNDER THE LORDSHIP OF CHRIST

If a pen doesn't write, what do you do with it? People have interesting responses. Some shake it. Some lick it. Some burn it. Some keep it. Most toss it. (We have an entire drawer at our house for pens that don't write.) Whatever you would do, we all agree that if it doesn't write, even if it's an expensive pen, it is not accomplishing its purpose.

Your life is your ministry. If it doesn't work, then you are not accomplishing your purpose. You can have all of the high-tech toys, big budgets, nice facilities, even a new church bus, but without a life worth imitating, all of that goes down the tube.

Think of it this way: our primary role in youth ministry is to be a model, an example for kids. "OK, tell me something new." What's new is what that really means. The Apostle Paul expresses it clearly in 1 Timothy 1:5, "The goal of this command is love, which comes from a pure heart and a good conscience and a sincere faith."

What's the goal? Love. What do we model? Perfection? Performance? External behavior? No. As my friend Dave Busby says: "It's a matter of the heart." We model love. The apostle describes it here as agape love. Is there anything that kids need today more than love?

Picture God as a big faucet. Agape love means that He has turned on the big faucet and is letting the love flow. Since He is the source of love (1 John 4:8), it never stops flowing. And I need to let it continually flow on me. Problem! I don't do that. I put the lid on the bucket.

That takes us to the second meaning of agape. God pours out His love, but I need to receive it. If I don't, it doesn't change my heart. Jesus expressed the issue well in John 14:21, "Whoever has my commands and obeys them, he is the one who loves me. He who loves me will be loved by my Father, and I too will love him and show myself to him." As I open my heart up to Christ, and obey Him, then His love will pour through me. I will experience the Father's love continually.

At this point the third meaning of agape kicks in. If God has poured out His love and I am responding with obedience that allows His love to flow through me, then that love will flow right on out to others. We won't have to try to splash a drop of love here and an ounce of love there, but rather it will flow all around, touching every life that my life touches. John was right: "We love because he first loved us."

What is at issue here is this: How do I become a channel of God's love? The Apostle Paul answers that in three phrases in 1 Timothy 1:5.

A pure heart. The apostle has two meanings in mind concerning a pure heart. First, he is thinking of a *clean heart.* The picture in Paul's mind is a spotless dish.

At our house we leave early most every morning. If the cereal bowl doesn't get put in the dishwasher, then the sun bakes that cereal onto the bowl so that the bowl almost needs an air hammer to clean it later that night. Score one for Paul. We are to confess sins quickly before they harden on us. The writer of Proverbs expressed it this way: "He who covers his sin shall not prosper; but he who confesses it and forsakes it shall receive mercy" (Prov. 28:13).

Do you have anything in your life right now that keeps you from having a clean heart?

Second, Paul is thinking of a *single heart,* meaning "unmixed motives." To have a pure heart means that my whole heart desires to know God and to love Him. It is the kind of attitude the psalmist expressed in Psalm 63:1, "O God, you are my God, earnestly I seek you; my soul thirsts for you, my body longs for you."

Count Zinzendorf, the eighteenth-century German Christian leader, was a man like this. Young, intelligent, well-educated, and affluent, he said, "I have but one passion; it is He, He alone."

No wonder the Lord used him to start a movement that would send more than one percent of all of the missionaries ever sent in church history. He discipled Peter Bohler, who influenced John Wesley in a way that caused Wesley to have his heart "strangely warmed" at Aldersgate. Zinzendorf started a prayer meeting that lasted 24 hours a day for 100 years. God used him because he had "but one passion."

Are there good things in your life, but not the best? Is there anything that keeps you from having an all out passion for God?

A good conscience. The apostle speaks of a good conscience to mean having no wrong relationships—not with parents, brothers and sisters, children, fellow church members, former friends, employers, employees, or teachers.

In Acts 24:16, Paul expresses it another way: "So I always take pains to have a clear conscience toward God and toward men."

One Sunday afternoon I was working on a science poster on our patio. I asked my little sister to get me a drink. I was 16. She was 13. She brought the drink. But I didn't take it. Finally she dumped it all over my almost-finished science poster. I was ticked. I stood up and slapped her. She ran inside. I ran after her. I was going to hit her again. From that point our relationship drifted apart. I could never do anything right for her. It was always the wrong size, the wrong date. Some time later when my sister was going through some problems, she told my mom, "Barry has been a crummy big brother to me." When my mom told me, it broke my heart. I knew I needed to get that right.

One night I visited my sister at her apartment. We sat on opposite ends of the couch. I said to her, "Cathey, I have been a crummy big brother to you." I listed several reasons why. Then I said, "Will you forgive me?" She sat there for a moment. Then, with big tears in her eyes, she slipped across the couch and put her arms around me. We hugged and cried.

All the barriers came down, and within six weeks I was able to help her directly with the problem she was facing. If my pride had stood in the way, I would have cut off the possibility of helping her and could have ruined her life.

Do you have any relationships that you need to straighten out—either to ask forgiveness or to extend forgiveness?

A sincere faith. The ancient idea of sincerity was "without wax." In those times sculptors would arrive in town and create a piece of art. Someone would buy it and decorate his home with it. But every now and then a pretender would arrive. He would break off a nose or an elbow from the sculpture and replace it with a wax nose or elbow. A person would buy the sculpture, assuming it was the real thing, but when he got home and the sun shone on it, the nose or elbow would fall off. It was a worthless piece of junk.

To be sincere is to be without wax. It means no hypocrisy. Total obedience expresses the idea pretty well.

In the church today we need to get our obedience level up to our knowledge level. When we do we will be sincere. One friend of mine says it this way: "You put into practice what you believe every day. All the rest is just religious talk."

That became a reality to me several years ago when I was leading a conference for youth leaders. The Lord was trying to speak to me. I had refused to deal with one issue because of the pain and embarrassment of it. But every time the speaker mentioned sin, the Lord brought this issue to mind. Finally it became clear that God would not use me anymore unless I became sincere on this situation.

I had cheated on some tests when I was in college. With all of the courage I could muster, I confessed this to God, to my understanding wife, and to this group of youth workers. But the hardest part of all was calling that professor. I'll always remember the day I went into my office to call him. I was so nervous. When I talked my voice was shaking. I said, "Sir, when I was in your class I cheated on some tests. That was wrong. I want to ask you to forgive me." He did. And I almost floated out of the room. Because I had sincerely obeyed, I never had to deal with that issue again. Nor did I ever have to hide from it. The shades were opened. The light was let in. It was dealt with.

Do you have any areas of disobedience in your life?

The love of God is already flowing. When we unclog the channel, His love can flow through us. The channel gets unclogged when we honestly let God search our hearts to discover any place where we don't have a pure heart, a good conscience, or a sincere faith.

Your life is a most valuable tool in God's hands. Like the pen, you have a purpose. When His love flows freely through an unclogged channel, He will accomplish His purpose of using you to change the lives of others.

BUILDING A LEADERSHIP TEAM OF VOLUNTEERS

The church always struggles with the leadership crunch. "Somebody please take the 10th-grade boys class." No one responds because the last person who had the 10th-grade boys had his house rolled every Friday night. Most lay youth workers feel totally inadequate. Yet instead of training them, we give them unfulfilling tasks like keeping the kids out of the bushes on the retreat. At one point the church realizes, "We need something more for our youth." Then they hire you, Yogi Youth pastor, and expect you to do it all. "He's the youth pastor. That's what we hired him for."

With leadership defined simply as "influence," we can say with confidence that one of our major goals of ministry is *to train leaders to influence the younger generation.*

Without such a goal your ministry will never be more than mediocre, even if you are good with kids. Your success becomes your failure. Even if you are the "Pied Piper" with kids and scores of them love to be with you, there is only so much of you to go around. Soon you begin to feel it—out eight nights a week, your wife and kids saying, "Who is that man?" when you do come home.

On the other hand, with a leadership team your ministry potential is unlimited. You will train a multiplied number of skilled leaders for a personalized ministry to students.

The Leadership Team's Purpose. If you minister in a program-oriented church, you know that the church uses people up and spits them out. But in a relationally-oriented church a different dynamic exists. Let's look at what was on Jesus' heart as He prayed for His disciples then and now. He asked the Father that His disciples would be

- Committed to Christ
- Committed to one another
- Committed to a ministry to the world (students)

When you have your youth leaders together, what do you do with them? Is it administrative and program-oriented? Or is it geared to give spiritual nourishment and personal encouragement? Nobody wants to come to another meeting. If you even suggest it, they dig their heels in. Can you blame them? But a relational get-together isn't just another meeting.

Bob was a dental student at Emory University in Atlanta. I had led him into a committed walk with Christ. He decided to come to our "Leadership Family" after I challenged him to be a part. In the meetings he was pretty quiet, until one night. That night Sandy came in late with tears in her eyes. She had just found out that her mother had cancer. Bob was sitting beside her. For the first time he reached out to minister to someone else. He prayed the sweetest prayer for Sandy. It was a precious moment. That experience was the catalyst that got him going. The group proved to be a very special experience for him. So much so that when he set up his dental practice, he called me and

41

said, "Barry, that time of growth meant so much to me that I want to do all of the dental work for you and your family for just what it costs me as long as I am in practice here." And that is exactly what he does!

Once members of your leadership team come a few times to a meeting that is geared to meet their needs, you won't be able to keep them away.

Doing the Ministry of Jesus. Jesus took his disciples through a four-phase process over the three years he was with them.

I do it. Jesus set the pace.

I do it and they are with me. Jesus almost always took his disciples "with him."

They do it and I am with them. Jesus let his disciples try the ministry that He did every day.

They do it and I am in the background to encourage. Jesus left his Holy Spirit to empower them to do the very ministry He did.

What is "it"? What did He teach them to do? What He did. And what did He do? To discover that, let's do a progressive Bible study. Look up the following verses and write down what Jesus did.

Isaiah 61:1. When the promised Messiah came, He would

(1) _____

(2) _____

(3) _____

Look at verses 2 and 3 for the incredible results, especially as applied to kids today.

Luke 4:18-19. Vaguely familiar? Now the Messiah has come to do what?

(1) _____

(2) _____

(3) _____

Turn the pages of the Gospels. Jesus does the very things He said He would do.

Mark 6:12-13. Ah ha! Now the disciples are doing what Jesus did. And what was that?

(1) _____

(2) _____

(3) _____

John 14:12. Now for the big kicker. What will we do that Jesus had been doing?

(1) _____

(2) _____

(3) _____

What a promise for you, your youth leaders and even your junior high kids!

We have the incredible privilege of doing the ministry of Jesus! And we get to raise up volunteer leaders, and they, in turn, raise up young people to do the same. If that doesn't fit your theological mold, then break out of it long enough to look at the kids described in chapter 1. Without salvation, healing, and deliverance how can they possibly come out of their pain and into wholeness?

No dull administrative meeting here. When leaders themselves begin to practice ministry as Jesus did it, they won't be able to wait to get together to report on the things that God has done. When that happens not only will you have a powerful spiritual dynamic at work, but also you will have reproduced yourself by the number on your leadership team. Powerful, multiplied ministry will be taking place.

DISCIPLING STUDENTS FOR MATURITY AND MINISTRY

When I talk to youth leaders I hear the same refrains over and over again.

- "I can't get my kids motivated."

- "They will come for concerts and fun, but. . . ."

- "Our group has no interest in Bible study and spiritual things."

Most of that has to do with our focused vision for our kids. Do you know what you want to come out at the other end of the tube? When kids are with you from 7th grade through 12th grade, what are you trying to produce?

To answer that, let's go back to what we decided earlier. Our goal is to produce *life change* and *life changers*. That doesn't start at an event. For it to happen we have to have a long-range plan. Not one that moves kids from event to event, but one that moves them through a week-to-week process of spiritual growth. Some of you are saying, "But I don't have any (or many) young people who want that." Yes, you do. They just don't know it yet.

If you set up a ministry of discipleship based on the principles of 2 Timothy 2:1-2, you *will* have kids to disciple: "You then, my son, be strong in the grace that is in Christ Jesus. And the things you have heard me say in the presence of many witnesses entrust to reliable men who will also be qualified to teach others."

Principle #1: Receiving Grace. Why do so many students who grow up in church drop out at about age 16? Why do so many kids walk out the door to go to college, leave their "religious bag" behind, and go absolutely berserk when they get to college? Simple. The church has communicated to kids that following Jesus is rules and religion and not a dynamic relationship with the living God.

Grace is God's supernatural ability in us through the Cross and the resurrection. All believers have the dynamic resurrection life of Jesus living in them through the Holy Spirit.

Discipleship can easily become legalistic. "I don't listen to rock music or chew tobacco." "I memorized four verses—how many did you memorize?" When we disciple kids, we must appeal to that embryonic Spirit living in each one of them—even the 8th-graders. (We could do a chapter on the subject "Do 8th Graders Have Souls," but we'll save that for a later book.) When we appeal to kids on the basis of internal conviction rather than external behavior, we are operating on the basis of grace and not legalism. *Discipleship creates an atmosphere where we trust the capability of the Holy Spirit to speak to each person in the group.*

Principle #2: Relationship Investment. The Apostle Paul says, "You ...me." A relationship existed between him and Timothy. Paul knew that *discipleship is investing your life in close personal relationships with others.*

When I led my first discipleship group I wasn't aware of that definition. I led the group like a classroom situation with the chairs lined up, weekly lecture, and the whole bit. After we stopped at the end of twelve weeks, I found out that one of the boys had started going to the Jewish synagogue and attending confirmation classes. Joining the synagogue was not my goal for the discipleship group! So I decided to get with Lee. We began to talk. I discovered that he had low self esteem, and that he had never really committed his life to Christ. I led him to Christ. As I learned about investing in relationships, I really did disciple him this time–through high school and college. Several years ago he called me on Thanksgiving night to tell me how grateful he was that I had taken the time to invest my life in his–that it had made an eternal difference. When I hung up the phone I yelled, "Yes! This is what the ministry is all about!" Lee Grady is now the editor of *Charisma* magazine. He grew as I invested in the relationship. Your kids will grow the same way.

Principle #3: Reflecting Christ's Character. Paul uses the word *entrust*. It means a sacred trust. It is like going to the safety deposit box at the bank. (All of you rich youth pastors identify with this illustration.) You have your key and the banker has his key. It takes both keys to get out all of your stocks, bonds, securities, silver holdings or maybe just your baseball cards. In the same way, when we disciple someone, we bring our lives and the young person brings his or her life and we enter into a partnership in the Spirit. Each one puts his key in, and that opens up the riches of Christ.

Discipleship is *a partnership in the Spirit to produce the character of Christ in the lives of others.*

What changes lives? We can teach *information*, but we know people who have been hearing the Bible every week for 40 years and yet they are no different. We can train in *skills* like quiet time and Scripture memory, and that is good, but it doesn't get to the heart of the matter. What changes lives is when we build *character* through applying grace in the context of relationships. Only then will kids be motivated to go after God and to reach their friends for Christ. Only then will they go out with a *mission*.

Be aware that this takes time. Miles Stanford said, "It takes six months to grow a squash, but it takes a lifetime to grow an oak tree." Do you want to produce squash or oak trees?

Principle #4: Reality Living. Using the phrase "many witnesses," Paul's meaning is "many life situations." *Discipleship only works in real life situations.*

This stark reality hit home with me one night when I had asked Kent, a young man I was discipling, to help me move some furniture. We moved a hide-a-bed away from the wall. Cookies, molded raisins, toys and other "stuff" were behind there. If you have children, you understand this. If you don't, then you don't have a clue. Kent looked at me as if to say *What is this junk?* We moved this piece, then opened it to check it. All the stuffing in the back fell out. Kent looked again, as if to say *cheap furniture.* Then we tried to move a 86" x 37" couch through a door that was 79" x 29". We pushed and pulled. We sweated. Kent jammed my finger against the wall. I let him know how bad it hurt. Then he scraped my newly painted wall with the couch, scarring both. At this point I really lost it and had a few choice words for him. We never did get the couch through the door. In fact, I was so frustrated I refused to touch it for two weeks.

Whatever spiritual pedestal I was on with Kent before, I fell off that night. But I learned some valuable lessons. First, I'm not perfect, and kids don't expect me to be. Second, all of the ground is level at the foot of the Cross. No Christian is in a higher class than another Christian, no matter what the age or maturity difference. Third, when I am human, kids can identify with me. They say, "If he fails at some things, maybe I can live the Christian life too." Fourth, Jesus is the master discipler. I'm not the big-time discipleship leader; rather Jesus is the one who is discipling us both to be more like Him. That night 2 Corinthians 12:9 came home to me: "[God says] My grace is sufficient for you. [I say with Paul] I will all the more gladly boast in my weakness that the power of Christ may rest upon me."

Principle #5: Recruiting Reliable People. When the Apostle Paul makes reference to "reliable men" he has in mind what some have called **FAT** people—**F**aithful, **A**vailable, and **T**eachable. In other words we are looking for students to disciple who are 100 percent sold out. They have the hunger and desire of the psalmist: "As the deer pants for streams of water so my soul pants for you, O God. My soul thirsts for God, for the living God" (Ps. 42:1-2).

You say: "Big problem! I don't know any kids like that." That's because most kids are like I was in adolescence. I was the kind of kid that youth leaders loved to hate. I disrupted every meeting, chased girls all over the church, got into pencil fights. (I still have scars in my arm and on my back side.) One of the deacons told my dad once: "Your

46

son is either going to be in prison or a preacher, and the verdict is still out on which one." Why was that? None of the principles we have discussed were applied to me. I had huge amounts of unchanneled energy. And I was underchallenged.

It does no good to insist that kids come up to our level. What we have to do to produce "reliable" disciples is to begin with them where they are, peel back the layers, and get into their hearts. *Discipleship works best when we accept students where they are, and take them where they need to be.*

Principle #6: Reproducing by Multiplication. In 2 Timothy 2:2 we find four generations of disciplemaking—Paul, Timothy, reliable men, others also. We can conclude from this that *disciplemaking by multiplication is God's best way to fulfill the Great Commission.*

Bill attended Georgia Tech. I met him during his sophomore year and, soon after, began to disciple him. A few months later he met John. Bill ate a hamburger with him every week before a class they had together. Through their friendship Bill led John to Christ and then began to disciple him. That continued on into the summer while they were both on a student exchange program in the former Soviet Union.

One Sunday they attended the Moscow Baptist Church. After the service a young Russian approached them. He had heard that they were Americans, and he wanted to speak English with them. In the conversation Bill and John discovered that Eugene had come to church because he was searching for meaning and purpose in life.

Bill and John took Eugene back to their room and John spent the rest of the day talking to Eugene about Christ. However, Eugene was not ready to make that kind of serious decision. But a few months later Bill and John got a letter that said in part, "I cannot wait to tell you about a magnificent experience I had. I repented on August 18 and received the Lord. . . . It is through your effort that another prodigal son has returned to the Father in heaven."

Later Eugene Grosman was granted an exit visa, came to the United States, and studied Bible and communications. In the last years of Communism he spoke on a radio program that reached between 10 and 15 million people each day in the former Soviet Union. One of the highlights of my life happened last year when I gave this illustration to 300 youth leaders we were training in Moscow. I had the privilege of having Eugene Grosman as my translator.

If each one of us will bloom where we are planted and design a strategy to disciple the young people where we are, then we will take giant strides toward fulfilling the Great Commission.

PENETRATING THE CAMPUS THROUGH RELATIONSHIPS

Emory, a youth pastor in Texas, went through our training. At first it made no sense to him. Then about the third day the lights came on. It changed his thinking so much that he called his pastor and apologized for wasting the church's time. He went back and soon began to go to the school campus. When he walked into the gym he saw one student named John sitting by himself in the bleachers. He talked to him that day on the campus. Later Emory invited him to an outreach event, then led him to Christ. John went through the process of discipleship, leadership training, and internship. Today he is youth pastor of a youth group of 600 students. It all started with one youth pastor penetrating the campus.

In order to penetrate the campus we need to know our objective:

Going where young people are

To build relationships

For the purpose of sharing the Gospel.

It takes a special commitment to go where students are. Adults who are willing to do that have a calling that involves some special desires.

A desire to be with young people. Like Jesus' desire to "pitch his tent among us" (John 1:14), we need to have a desire to move out of the secure, comfortable environment of the adult world into the world of the school campus and local hangouts.

After visiting a campus one youth leader reflected: "The thought of going into their territory is a little overwhelming. It can be a little scary when you begin wondering if they'll accept or reject you. But when I got there I was surprised at how many new relationships could be built by just being on campus."

A desire to win the friendship of young people. Being on the campus does not mean jumping on the cafeteria table and thumping our Bibles. Rather, we spend time with students building friendships. Paul expressed the significance of this approach when he said, "So being affectionately desirous **of you, we gave you not only the gospel, but our very own lives as well"** (1 Thess. 2:8).

As you show concern for students as individuals, learning of their interests and needs, not only will your friendships deepen, but you will discover the points of pain in their lives and be able to apply the Gospel to them. As one youth leader put it: "[This] gives us credibility with students who are outside of our church. If the only time they see us is on Sunday, it is easy for them to think that we don't understand what's going on in their lives and therefore don't care about them. Our being on campus makes students feel like they are important to us."

A desire to see young people come to know Jesus. Availability on the campus and sensitive relationships focused on the needs of students eventually provide the opportunity to share Christ openly. Moving from building the relationship to sharing Jesus will come from a heart's desire that Paul expressed in Romans 10:1: "My heart's desire and prayer to God for the Israelites is that they may be saved." One youth leader described his motivation this way: "Nothing is quite as exciting as sitting down with a student one to one and telling him about Jesus Christ and then helping him ask Jesus into his life."

Students today have a tremendous need for love. They are crying out through all sorts of weird behavior for real relationships with people who care, and ultimately for a relationship with Jesus who will make them whole.

DESIGNING OUTREACH EVENTS TO DRAW KIDS TO CHRIST

When all of the other essentials of excellent youth ministry are in place, then, and only then, the time is right to put this essential into operation. The information you need for designing outreach events you have in your hand now. Read on!

This brief discussion of the five essentials of excellence is only an introduction. For more information and materials on how you can make these strategic principles operative in your situation write or call:

Reach Out Ministries
3961 Holcomb Bridge Road #200
Norcross, GA 30092
(404) 441-2247

Lay these tracks before you burn yourself out trying to put on events that are not connected to a process.

ACTION POINT

1. Order the video on "The Reach Out Strategy" from Reach Out Ministries by calling (404) 441-2247. Request a video manual to be sent.

2. Go through the video yourself, and then call us with any questions or problems.

3. Fill out the "Five Essentials For Excellence" sheet on page 186 of "The Outreach Event Planner."

4. Take your volunteer leaders on a vision retreat and challenge them to implement this strategy with you. End the retreat by giving them the opportunity to become part of your leadership family.

5. With your team, implement *the practical steps* of this strategy. As you do you will lay the tracks you need to run on in order to make your outreach events successful.

Four

Strike the Deadly Blow:
Smashing Resistance with Prayer

At our church we had started the youth ministry from scratch. In about two years we had 125 kids coming to an apartment clubhouse every week for an outreach event. We had moved out of one place and into another because so many kids were coming. Every week we had a high-energy meeting that kids really enjoyed. About 70 percent of them were non-Christians from the Stone Mountain campus. However with all of the positive things happening, we noticed that many of the kids were resistant to the Gospel. The ones who did receive Christ didn't seem to stick with it. Even some of the stronger Christians were struggling.

After scratching our heads over the situation for a period of time, we finally figured out what the problem was. *We had created all of this without serious prayer.* We then had an all-out prayer focus that included the entire church. Three weeks after we began this intense prayer effort, the resistance to the Gospel disappeared. Kids started coming to Christ. We had seventeen in one month who became Christians. Sixteen of those stuck with Christ over the long haul. The older Christians began to have a new hunger. Because we struck a big blow through prayer, the whole ministry turned in a fresh new direction.

To do excellent outreach events you must strike a big blow through prayer. That means involving yourself, your leaders, and your students in a powerful prayer strategy that will rock Satan's socks—turning back the kingdom of darkness and bringing in the kingdom of light. When

51

people gather in prayer your group is poised with that powerful weapon that smashes Satan's resistance and releases kids from their indifference and hardness. As you persevere, God will enable you to conduct your outreach events in a way that produces lasting fruit and not just energized fluff.

PRAYER MOMENTUM

John Bunyan, the author of *Pilgrim's Progress* and a powerful man of prayer, said: "You can do more than pray after you've prayed, but you cannot do more than pray until you have prayed."[1]

That statement sets our priorities for us. The better part of our energy for an outreach event needs to go toward prayer. In order to do that it is essential to have an on-going prayer strategy for your overall ministry but specifically for your outreach events. Two resources by Victor Books provide an overall strategy for you:

(1) *Penetrating the Campus*, Barry St. Clair and Keith Naylor. Chapter 3, "Bending Your Knees on Campus."

(2) *Taking Your Campus for Christ*, Barry St. Clair and Keith Naylor. Chapter 5, "Passionately Romantic," and chapter 6, "Ultimately the Power Weapon."

To develop a specific strategy for your outreach event, let's focus on Jeremiah 33:3, "Call to me and I will answer you and tell you great and unsearchable things you do not know." Out of this great verse God gives three practical prongs for a prayer strategy that we can use for our outreach events.

The Prayer. The Lord says, "Call to me." God pleads with us to do this, but we spend so little time at it. As a result, we cut off God's presence and power and are left to do God's work man's way. David Bryant in *Concerts of Prayer* suggests four reasons that keep people from making prayer a priority.

Lack of appreciation. Often people just don't have a sense of how awesome God is. Jeremiah recognized God's awesome power when he said, "Ah, Sovereign Lord, You have made the heavens and the earth by your great power and outstretched arm. Nothing is too hard for you" (Jer. 32:17). The more we understand the awesomeness of God the more we will pray.

Lack of desperation. As programs fail and burnout sets in, I've observed that youth leaders become more desperate. One veteran youth worker who has a huge youth group and all the high-tech gadgets that go with it, told me: "With all we have, none of it helps kids respond to God unless we as leaders are coming to God continually in total and utter dependence." That attitude unleashes God's unlimited resources to work in our behalf. We need to cry out, like the psalmist, "My soul thirsts for God, for the living God. When can I go and meet with God?" (Ps. 42:2).

Lack of dedication. People would pray more if they were more whole-hearted toward God's cause. God is not going to entrust His power and kingdom resources into the hands of someone who is not 100 percent sold out to Jesus Christ and His cause. Our degree of dedication needs to fall in line with what Jesus laid out for us, "If anyone would come after me, he must deny himself and take up his cross daily and follow me" (Luke 9:23).

Lack of conviction. Maybe you have never seen God work in powerful answer to prayer. Or maybe you prayed for something and it just didn't happen the way you had hoped. You might think, "I know God *can*, I wonder if He *will?*" Since faith is "the assurance of things hoped for, the conviction of things not seen" (Heb. 11:1), ask God now for one thing you can trust Him for that will build your conviction that He is able.

If you realize the need to have a stronger prayer emphasis in your personal life and in your ministry, the solution is to pray. S. D. Gordon challenges us:

> The great people of the earth today are the people who pray. I do not mean those who talk about prayer; nor those who say they believe in prayer; but I mean those people who take time and pray. These are the people today who are doing the most for God: in winning souls; in solving problems; in awakening churches; in keeping the old earth sweet awhile longer.[2]

Jesus gave us that same challenge in Matthew 7:7-8: "Ask and it will be given to you; seek and you will find; knock and the door will be opened to you. For everyone who asks receives; he who seeks finds; and to him who knocks, the door will be opened."

Specifically what Jesus desires for us to do in prayer is this:

Ask. Align yourself with God by agreeing with him. "Father, I want what you want." Then the only thing outside the reach of your prayers is anything outside the will of God.

Seek. Stand for others. Align yourself with those who cannot pray for themselves: family, friends, kids from broken homes, and secular kids who do not know Christ.

Knock. Press on for a change. Persistently pound on the door. When you knock with perseverance it means that you have a burden in prayer. "Father, You must act, and I will pray until You bring about a change." Pursue God relentlessly until His will is carried out fully.

This kind of prayer is illustrated by my friend whose son was running away from Christ. Bob told his son that he was going to fast and pray until his son came back to Christ. He did that for several weeks, and his son responded. That's the kind of prayer you need for your outreach events—serious, persistent prayer.

The Promise. God's promise "I will answer you" gets repeated over and over again in the Bible. And on what condition does God fulfill His promise? The condition that we abide in Him. Jesus rephrases the Jeremiah 33:3 prayer when He says, "If you remain [abide] in me, and my words remain in you, ask whatever you wish, and it will be given you." Why is that so? Because what we want will be what God wants. When we pray according to His promise, and He answers according to His promise, then the result is that we will bear much fruit and glorify the Father" (v. 8).

Sometimes God answers quickly. When Bobby called me on Thursday and asked me if I would come over to his house and pray for him on Sunday, I said I would. He told me that the doctor had found cancer in his foot and leg and that they were going to amputate his leg at the knee the next Thursday. That Sunday I went to his house. His family gathered around and we prayed. We laid hands on him and anointed him with oil. His son-in-law prayed a particularly fervent prayer. On Thursday the doctors took a slice of his toe to do a pathological report before they took off the lower leg. They found some cancer cells. Then they took another slice and found none. Upon further research they found that the cancer had disappeared! That was over three years ago. When I saw Bobby the other day, I asked him how he was doing. "One hundred percent," he said.

Sometimes God doesn't seem to be in a hurry. Some prayers I've prayed for months or years, and it doesn't seem that they have an answer yet. But the Bible says that "God is not slow as some count slowness" (2 Pet. 3:9). He is on a different clock. My father-in-law prayed for the salvation of one man in his city every week for eighteen years. He saw him every week and witnessed to him many times. No response. Then in the eighteenth year, the man turned around and came to Christ.

I don't pretend to understand how God works on these things. But I do know that He has made some pretty amazing promises to us. And so often the issue is that "we have not because we ask not" (James 4:2).

The Potential. If we know that God is going to show us and tell us "great and unsearchable things you do not know," then what is the limit to our prayers? The only limit is the narrowness of our vision and the smallness of our prayers. Billy Graham said that we cannot expect great answers to prayer unless we offer great prayers for God to answer.

As you look at your situation and consider what you want to happen at your outreach events, clarify what you are praying toward. Two sweeping themes of the New Testament provide direction.

Pray for God to fulfill the Great Commandment. Jesus told us that the greatest commandment was to "love the Lord your God with all your heart . . . and to love your neighbor as yourself" (Matt. 22:37-38). Pray that an attitude of loving God and loving others will sweep your group, but also the schools, the hate groups, the gangs, the druggies, the partiers, and other groups.

Pray for God to fulfull the Great Commission. When Jesus said, "Go, therefore, and make disciples of all nations" (Matt. 28:19-20), certainly He was not teasing us with the impossible. Because "all nations" are on God's heart, we need to have that on our hearts, too. Pray for the evangelization of the world, starting with the students in your youth group and at the high schools in your community.

Frank Laubach, the renowned literacy advocate, said that "prayer is the mightiest force on earth." If enough of us prayed enough we could see God's will done "on earth as it is in heaven." If you have enough people praying enough in your situation, then God will move heaven and earth on your behalf.

In a practical application of Jeremiah 33:3, let's develop a two-level prayer strategy for your outreach events.

PRAYER POWER TEAMS

The concept of the Prayer Power Team comes from Matthew 18:18-20—"where two or three come together in my name." When we pray according to these verses, getting into groups of two and three, He comes into the group and makes His presence and power available to us. He moves all of heaven and earth on our behalf. Then He sends us out in His name "to bind and loose," to be the answer to our own prayers. Incredible!

To build a student prayer base for your outreach events you will want to challenge your kids to pray in Prayer Power Teams. Keith Naylor and I challenged students on how to do this in *Taking Your Campus for Christ.*

3 Friends Meeting

3 Times a Week to Pray for

3 Friends Who Need Christ

You can use the same challenge with your kids.

PRAYER PACESETTERS

Before we can ask kids to pray, we as adult leaders need to set the pace for them. If it doesn't happen with us, it will never happen with them. We need to take the same challenge that they take—to become a part of a Prayer Power Team.

The concept is the same, with a few twists unique to youth leaders.

3 Friends Meeting

3 Times a Week to Pray for

3 Friends Who Need Christ

3 Friends Meeting. Write down your name and the names of two other youth leaders with whom you would like to pray. If you are a professional youth leader then I highly recommend praying with youth leaders from another church, preferably with someone from another denomination. That will begin to build unity and a network with other churches so when you are ready to do a multichurch magnet event you will have the relationships and the spiritual base in prayer.

3 Times a Week to Pray. Write down the best times for you to pray. You can arrange your schedule however you want. If it is better to meet once a week for an hour, you can. Or if it will work better for you and the other youth leaders, you can meet three times a week. You might consider meeting early at the school to pray, implementing some of the creative ideas mentioned later in the chapter. (For a prayer format, see chapter 3 of *Penetrating the Campus.*) Feel free to flex here. Whatever you do, confirm it with your other two friends.

3 Friends Who Need to Know Christ. You can start by praying for three lost kids each, but then you will want to expand your praying. Focus your praying in two areas:

(1) Pray for spiritual awakening among the Christians on the campus. As you pray for Christian students by name, envision them praying, serving, and witnessing lovingly and boldly.

(2) Pray for lost students. Pray for them by name. You can use a yearbook to pray for a wide variety of kids. Pray that a movement of God's Spirit will sweep across the campus drawing young people to Christ.

MEGA IDEAS FOR CREATIVE PRAYING

To keep prayer a central focus for the outreach events, you can use these creative ideas or put together your own unique approach for your situation. Instead of taking responsibility for all of this yourself, you will want to set up the Prayer Team as discussed in chapter 9.

Set up a 12- or 24-hour prayer chain with students signing up for 15-minute segments. If you have enough students involved in the Prayer Power Teams you could have each team take a 30- or 45-minute segment. You might try this for a limited time period, like a week before a big event. Then if it goes well, expand it.

• Have each student make a "Top Ten" list of the ten friends they most want to come to Christ. Have them pray in small groups for some of those each week at your youth group meeting. This will keep in front of each student the issue of the need for their friends to know Christ, even the ones who don't have that burden now.

• Pray over the room you will meet in. Assign a different group of kids each week to come and pray. Have a format or a prayer list of the different items you want them to pray for. Invite the presence and power of God into the room.

• Gather all of the Christians on the campus for prayer once a month. You can involve several other youth leaders in this with you. Meet at a neutral site close to the campus.

• A parents' off-campus prayer meeting can draw together concerned Christian parents in that one school. This will afford an opportunity for parents to meet each other. One of them could carry on the prayer meeting from there. Each time you have an event you could mobilize them to pray for that particular school.

• During your event set up a prayer wall of parents, youth leaders and kids who surround the entire room or building praying for the meeting as it is happening.

• Use a Target Prayer Strategy. In the room where you have your youth group, but not where the outreach event is being held, have the kids and leaders write the initials of the three people they are praying for in their Prayer Power Teams on a "prayer bullet" (a paper identification tag available in an office supply store). Have them write their names on the other side. Then each student pins the tags to the outer ring of a target you have put in place. Once the student has shared the Gospel with his non-Christian friend, he moves the bullet to the next circle. When that person accepts Christ, the bullet is moved to the center of the target and turned over, so the name of the new Christian faces out. This visual target creates excitement about and encouragement to pray for and share with lost kids.[3] Build prayer into the HIT Team meetings (see chapter 9). Each team that is responsible for one area of the outreach event can build prayer into its preparation for the event. Either keep prayer on the agenda of the HIT Team leaders or appoint a person on each HIT Team to be responsible for prayer.

• Set up a prayer walk. This can take several different forms. It can be done by parents, youth leaders and/or students. When the people arrive, divide them into teams. At this point you can choose between two options. (1) Assign each team to a school. They will go to the school and walk around each building praying for God's presence and power to operate there. (2) All of the teams together can do a Jericho

Walls March. The teams march seven times around the building where the outreach event will be held. As they march each team has different prayer assignments—the set-up, the music, kids to come, and so on.

• Invite kids to prayer parties the week of a special outreach event. The concept is the same as the cottage prayer meeting of generations past. Along with refreshments and fellowship, have a concentrated period of prayer for the event. Plan for several different locations so that kids can do this in their neighborhood or area of town.

• Design a prayer breakfast on the morning of the event or the day before. You can use this to build momentum for the event as well as communicate any information about the event. You might invite a speaker and have music, but the primary purpose is prayer.

• Use your Sunday School time to build a prayer emphasis. You can have students pray in small groups, or by classes. Having a prayer card with requests and information would be helpful to give to each teacher. This could be the place you use the Prayer Target.

• Give each student a card with a breakdown of each hour of the day (8:00 A.M. through 8:00 P.M.) and a prayer request listed beside each hour. They will have one issue to pray for each hour of the day of the event.

• Prepare a prayer calendar with one prayer request for each day of the month. Encourage the kids to carry the card in their wallet and pray for one request each day. A variation of this would be to prepare a small notebook quarterly that would include all of the prayer requests for the youth group that quarter. At the end of the month or quarter you can go back over each request and rejoice over the specific prayers answered.

• Start a Moms in Touch group that meets every week to pray for the youth ministry and particularly the outreach events.

• Prepare cards with the name and picture of each kid in the school. Add to each card any prayer requests for that student. Pass these out to parents who would be interested in praying for them.

• Hand out cards of each student in the youth group to senior adults (or even younger adults). Have them pray secretly for this one student all year. At the end of the year have a banquet that invites adults and kids together. At the banquet they share requests and answers over the whole year.

• Set up 40 days of prayer like in Acts 1-2. You might do this 40 days before you launch into doing outreach events on a regular basis, or before some particularly significant event.

• Include a prayer, a prayer reminder, or a prayer quote in your weekly or monthly mailout to the kids.

Well, no lack of ideas here! You can use some, any, all, or part of them for your outreach event. Do this keeping in mind that this prayer saturation isn't just to keep people occupied, but *to cover every aspect of your event in prayer so that the presence and power of God can be manifest in that meeting.*

ACTION POINT

Incorporating what you are already doing in the area of prayer, as well as what you have learned in this chapter, write out your prayer strategy for your outreach events. Include your personal strategy, a strategy for your leaders, and one for your students. The sheet to do that is on page 191 of "The Outreach Event Planner."

1. John Bunyan, "Reflections on Prayer," quoted in *Tabletalk* (February 1987), 5.

2. S. D. Gordon, *Quiet Talks on Prayer* (Westwood, N.J.: Fleming H. Revell, 1967), 11.

3. "Using a Prayer Target," in material created by Billy Beachum for Super Summer. For more information, write Student Discipleship Ministries, P.O. Box 6747, Ft. Worth, TX 76115.

Five

Ride the Big Wave:
Gathering People for High-Energy Momentum

Shawn did a good job in youth ministry. He had been at it for a few years. The church liked him and he liked the church. Then he went through the training highlighted in chapter 3. That put together some missing pieces of the puzzle for him. In his mind he sensed he had "the tracks to run on." He had taken the challenge to customize a prayer strategy for the youth ministry, too. In fact, when he got home he set aside two days of prayer to determine how all of this fit together in his situation. In those two days the wave began to gather strength, creating a high-powered momentum that would later crash the shore with great impact.

He began the two days by putting butcher paper all around the room. He wrote up the five essentials from chapter 3 and began to pray: "Lord, show me how everything I do fits around these five essentials." In the process of categorizing every activity and event, the Lord reminded him of seven people whose names he had written down during the training because he had offended them in some way. Immediately, he obeyed God, got up, made the contacts and asked forgiveness. He came back the next day with a fresh sense of God's presence. Now he was having fun! He got it all laid out, deciding what could stay and what needed to go. He set his priorities and made a timeline so he wouldn't feel he had to do it all at once.

For the next weekend Shawn had set up a vision retreat for all of his youth workers. Seventeen came. He began the retreat telling about how the Lord reminded him to call those seven people he had offended. He shared some of the significant results in those relationships. That set the tone for a time of confession, praise and prayer that lasted long into the evening. Shawn reported,

> God moved. We had a spiritual awakening right there. All seventeen committed themselves to be on our Leadership Team. Since then we have developed a prayer strategy, and a people strategy that is preparing our leaders and students to reach kids at school who need Christ and to bring them to our outreach events. We definitely have the momentum.

In order to design outreach events that gather and then maintain momentum, we must bring all of the key players together in unity. Everyone has to be on the same page. Several key individuals and groups have to move along together. Who are they? And how do they do that?

THE LEADER: THAT'S YOU!

Students need leaders. As the youth leader in your church, now more than ever before, you have the opportunity to lead not only Christian students, but secular students as well. In order for you to be prepared to take advantage of this vital opportunity, you must take some critical steps.

Define your philosophy of ministry with outreach to secular students in mind. Build into the heart of what you are doing an intense focus on lost kids. From reading the first several chapters you should have that clearly in your scope. The strategy discussed in chapter 3 will give evangelism its proper perspective and place in your ministry.

Of great importance is articulating this philosophy so you are not the only one who knows where you are going. Before you articulate it orally, you need to have it written down. Let's pause here to acknowledge that most youth leaders fly by the seats of their pants, operate off the cuff, wing it, are "led by the Spirit." (Which "spirit" is up for grabs.) So writing down your philosophy of ministry may not be number one on your list of favorite things to do. However, I am making a plea with you to write it. Not only write it, but refine it so that it is in an excellent form to explain to others. When you do that you will have a tool that will serve as your "north star." It will not only keep you on course, but also it will give direction to your pastor, adult leaders, and students. (See "The Outreach Event Planner" for a sample written philosophy.)

Expand your vision with your whole city in mind. Your outreach event will be limited only by the size of your vision. Before beginning, you need to see the potential from God's perspective. Leadership that imposes limits on God can, and has, stunted many outreach opportunities.

Maybe you have seen outreach as your kids bringing a few of their friends.

Maybe you have thought you would be successful if your group grew by, let's say, 20 in the next year.

Maybe you have looked at your youth group of 30 and haven't seen that your parish is the high school of 3,000 down the street.

Maybe you have seen one school, when ten schools exist in your city.

Maybe you have thought that your church could reach every student without considering how you can network with other churches.

Maybe you have thought that your denomination was the only one doing anything, without considering how you could be a partner with some churches of other denominations to get the vision accomplished.

Ask God to expand your vision so that you see yourself actively involved in reaching out to

Every kid

on every campus

in every community.

To get a handle on your vision, write down your wildest dreams concerning what God can do in your outreach events. Then condense your dreams into three or four sentences based on the following criteria: (1) Are my dreams consistent with my overall philosophy of ministry? (2) Are my dreams consistent with Scripture? (Support your main points with biblical principles or illustrations.) (3) Do I have the spiritual maturity that allows God to fulfill these dreams through me? (4) How do my pastor, church leaders and more spiritually mature friends evaluate my dreams?

Check out your dreams in all of these areas. After you have revised them, then adapt them into a solid, Scripture-based vision for outreach events. Now that you have God's vision, ask Him to fulfill it. Include it in your philosophy of ministry above.

Share ownership of the ministry with other leaders and students. This can't be your vision only. Others must know that they "own" the vision too. For all of you Star Trek fans, fulfill your fantasies and pretend you are Captain Kirk of the Starship Enterprise. You have Mr. Spock and all of the others under your command. Each one knows his ongoing mission: "to explore new worlds, to seek out new life and new civilizations and to boldly go where no one has ever gone before." Each one has his role in carrying out the mission. All work together to fulfill the mission and do whatever is necessary to defeat the Klingons.

Now that is the kind of focused, tight-knit team you want to build. In order to do that you have to share ownership of the mission. This does not mean that you turn all of the responsibility over to someone else. But it does mean that as you guide the direction of the ship, adult leaders and students will take major roles of responsibility in the mission. Wouldn't it be great to say "Beam me up, Scottie" and all of it would be done. That is where the analogy breaks down. (Maybe you think it already has.) To build a team that shares ownership takes mega-effort on your part. But it will take you "where no one has ever gone before" in your church and community.

Model a lifestyle of evangelism. Some youth workers fall into the do-what-I-say-not-what-I-do syndrome. This will not cut it with Christian kids, because they see right through it. Most of them are surrounded by more non-Christians than they will ever encounter again. Deep inside, most of them want to live for Christ and share their faith. Your role is to model that for them.

Picture your youth group like an arrow. You are the point of the arrow, setting the pace and providing direction. They are the shaft, following your lead. Some will be right behind you. Some will be "way back there." But they all need someone to look to, in order to know how to relate Christ to their friends and to share their faith on campus.

For them to be able to "walk the walk and talk the talk" they need someone who can set an example in "walking" and "talking" for them. I'm totally convinced that one of the primary reasons kids don't share their faith at school is that they have never seen anyone do it on a consistent basis. And so, quite frankly, they don't know how. Unless they have had someone model it and work with them to instill confidence, even something as simple as inviting a friend to an outreach event can scare them to death. One youth pastor, when asked why his kids boldly share Christ, responded: "They do it because I do it."

If your adult leaders and core kids don't have a heart for communicating Christ to their friends, and you have had contact with them long enough to influence them, you need to ask yourself some serious questions. Maybe their lack of zeal is reflected in your lack of zeal. But if you are setting the pace, you know that it is catching!

One youth pastor, going regularly to the campus and from there meeting with kids to communicate Christ, established a 13-week training course to help youth workers and kids share their faith. Over a two-year period more than 125 workers and kids completed this training. One parent of two teenagers, named Phil, had been a deacon and Sunday School teacher for 20 years but had always lacked the confidence to witness boldly. Anxious to overcome this weakness, he signed up for the course. This youth pastor had the opportunity to lead this man and guide him, even to take him out and let him see how the youth pastor communicated Jesus.

One afternoon Phil struck up a conversation with a 16-year-old runaway, Becky. She had returned home two days before after hitting rock bottom—strung out on drugs, malnourished, and pregnant. Much to Phil's surprise, Becky was eager and open to his "butchered" presentation of the Gospel and gave her heart to Jesus. In the year since she became a Christian she has completely recovered from her drug habit, given birth to a healthy baby girl, chosen to give the baby up for adoption, enrolled in school and become an honor student, and led six of her classmates to Christ. Now she is training others to share their faith.

In light of what we have discussed, ask yourself the question, "What do I, personally, need to do to get ready to lead others in producing these outreach events?"

THE PASTOR AND CHURCH LEADERSHIP: YOUR SUPPORT TEAM

In order to make this thing work over the long haul, you need the support of your pastor and church leadership. Good communication at this point and at this level will save you a lot of grief later on. To communicate effectively with your pastor and church leaders you will need to follow through on several important issues.

Pray for wisdom and insight. Before approaching the leadership of your church, recall the promise from Proverbs 2:6, "For the Lord gives wisdom, and from his mouth comes knowledge and understanding."

As you pray about how to present this to the leaders, ask the Lord to prepare you and them. He will give you specific insights into the situation and actions to take that will help you communicate properly.

A positive attitude will make a big difference here. You may have gone to the church leaders before and gotten burned. Or you may feel intimidated because you are so young. If you are thinking, *They won't listen to me,* then remember the promise of 1 Timothy 4:12: "Don't let anyone look down on you because you are young, but set an example for the believers in speech, in life, in love, in faith and in purity." You will be amazed at how far a positive attitude will take you in getting these issues worked out.

Another option is that the Lord wants to do some housecleaning in your life. That's always an option! One youth pastor complained to me that his pastor wouldn't let him do anything. Every time he tried to talk to his pastor he ran into a brick wall. He said he intimidated his pastor with his aggressiveness. But at a Reach Out Ministries conference the Lord revealed to him that he was the problem, not his pastor. Through this he faced the problem and confessed his sin. He told the pastor that he wanted to work on his team, supporting him, praying for him, and encouraging him. As a result the barriers came down and he and his pastor grew closer. Then, when a crisis hit their church, these two were able to stand together in a trusting relationship.

God wants to work in and through you as He prepares you to communicate.

Present your vision. When you meet with your church leadership, talk about two areas: (1) the needs of students generally, and those in your city particularly; and (2) the church's opportunity to meet those needs.

To show the needs of students, gather some national and local statistics and news articles on teenage issues in your community. Obviously the ultimate need is to know Jesus Christ. That will lead you into the second area.

Present your vision for ministry. Show how your vision will meet kid's needs. The last part of that should explain how the outreach events fit in. Prepare it so that it looks sharp. Get someone to do some graphics for it. This will communicate that you have thought through this thoroughly, that you know what you are talking about, and that you are serious about it. They will be impressed with your diligence and seriousness, and, therefore, will more likely trust you to carry out this vision. (Again, refer to "The Outreach Planner" for a sample.

To handle this properly, make an appointment with your pastor first. Explain everything to him one-to-one, getting his input privately. Get his direction on who you need to communicate to next. Set up that meeting and go through the same process with them.

Paint a realistic picture of what is involved. Help your pastor and church leaders see that secular students won't act like Christian students. Non-Christians act like non-Christians. We can't expect them to act any other way. Proverbs 14:4 gets the point across this way: "Where there are no oxen, the manger is empty, but from the strength of an ox comes an abundant harvest."

If you want a clean church, no cigarette butts in the parking lot, then don't invite lost students. Finding chewing gum on the carpet comes with the territory. But then, this proverb reminds us, if you don't take that risk, then don't expect new, young, vibrant believers in the church.

You might say to your leadership: "What is our focus? Is it a clean building and a calm, quiet atmosphere? If it is, we should never reach out to and invite secular kids. But if our focus is reaching the world for Jesus Christ, then we definitely need to invite and welcome all students—even if it means gum on the carpet."

Ask them to take the risk of being relevant. You are *not* asking the church leaders to compromise any basic bibical principles or convictions, but reaching lost kids probably will mean moving out of your comfort zone on some cultural issues. For example, one of the hot issues is music. If the outreach event is to be culturally relevant, then you will need to play music that the students enjoy. This outreach event is not for adults, but for kids. Just like the kids don't need to complain about the music in the adult meeting, the adults don't need to complain about the music in the kids' meeting.

If this music issue is particularly touchy, I would recommend that you read and then give to your pastor/leaders *The Contempory Christian Music Debate* (Tyndale House) by Steve Miller, who is on our staff in Eastern Europe. It is the most balanced treatment on the subject I've seen anywhere.

The fruit of seeing students come to know Christ is on the end of the limb. We have to climb up the ladder, away from all the church things that make us feel secure, and reach out to the end of the limb if we want to pick the fruit. It is never easy, it is always risky; but we have to choose between our comfortable security and picking the fruit in students' lives.

Invite their specific support. Ask your pastor and then the leaders to stand with you on what you present. Encourage them to make a verbal expression of support in three areas.

First, ask them to stand with you on the vision of ministry you presented.

Second, secure their prayers. Probably you will want to come up with one of the creative ideas from the prayer chapter, giving them a specific way to pray for you. You will experience greater success if you give them something written and then continue to supply reports and requests to them on an ongoing basis. The more consistently they pray for you, the more solidly they will support you.

Third, ask them for the finances you need. Be straightforward. Present your budget. (See "The Outreach Event Planner" for a sample budget. If budgeting is not your forte, get an accountant in your church to help you put the budget together so it will be realistic.) Ask them to provide the budget you need for one year, then you will sit down with them and evaluate what the ministry has accomplished and how it needs to be adjusted.

Do not hesitate. Do not back down. Be humble and loving, but also be confident. Find out if they are behind you or not. If they offer their support, thank them and move ahead with confidence. If they do not, ask questions and discover why. Listen. God will teach you through them. At all costs, continue to submit to the authority of their leadership. Avoid any rebellious attitude or action. Remember, God is in control. You can trust Him. Perhaps He is protecting you from starting something you are not quite ready for. Or you might realize that you are in a situation in which two competing philosophies exist. The Bible teaches, "Do two walk together unless they have agreed to do so?" (Amos 3:3).

If you discover that you have a conflict on philosophy, not personalities or methods, then you need to begin to ask the Lord to lead you to another situation where you and the leadership share the same vision. After the meeting you will have plenty of time to reflect on these heavy thoughts.

Invite the leaders to come. After gaining the support of your church leaders, give them the opportunity to come and observe what you are doing, especially at one of the outreach events. The more they are involved, the more they will be on your team.

THE LEADERSHIP TEAM: MOBILIZED FOR ACTION

Based on the assumption that you have assembled your leadership team and that you currently meet with them, we can move toward how to involve them strategically in outreach events. They will make the greatest contribution in two critical areas.

Building Relationships with Students. No effective outreach event takes place without a large network of relationships of Christians with non-Christians. Over the years the largest outreach events in the world have been the Billy Graham crusades. The heart and soul of their outreach strategy has been "Operation Andrew," which is based on John 1:40-42.

> Andrew, Simon Peter's brother, was one of the two who heard what John had said and who had followed Jesus. The first thing Andrew did was to find his brother Simon and tell him, "We have found the Messiah" (that is, the Christ). And he brought him to Jesus.

The leaders are the ones who will be the prime examples for your core kids in how to establish relationships with non-Christians. Rick Caldwell, who has done highly effective youth outreach events for several years, expresses the importance of this with these comments:

> I think most of us are being a bit idealistic when we expect large numbers of non-church-oriented pagan youth to flock to our weekly worship services, drop their emotional defenses, and embrace our messages with repentant hearts. Quite honestly, most non-church-oriented youth feel like fish out of water when they attend the average evangelical worship service...[or] even our high-energy youth meetings.

I contend that a non-church-oriented youth is like a newly captured animal in a cage. He is tense, on the defensive and frightened. His new environment threatens him and prevents him from being open or at ease.

The one element that can make a radical difference in the non-church-oriented youth's anxiety level is the security of a familiar face, especially if it belongs to a person that has cared enough to initiate and develop a personal relationship with him.

If we are to shoot through the emotional walls surrounding most non-church-oriented kids' hearts, we must use relationships as ammunition instead of religious rhetoric. This is perhaps the most challenging, but the most effective way to reach today's non–church-oriented young person.[1]

An entire book has been devoted to helping you and your volunteer leaders know how to go to the campus and build relationships with non-Christians. For specific help in this area read *Penetrating the Campus* by Barry St.Clair and Keith Naylor. One whole chapter discusses how to multiply your leaders in relationships.

Playing a Vital Role in the Outreach Meeting. For the outreach meeting itself, volunteer youth leaders help you set the pace. Going back to the illustration of the arrow we used earlier, you are the point, but your leadership team makes the point of the weapon larger and more powerful. If you have invested in them and multiplied yourself, then they will be able to do what you do. You have much more maturity, skill and manpower available when you have trained leaders to help you in this highly labor-intensive meeting.

Depending on abilities, spiritual gifts, and personal preferences, your leaders will have a wide variety of vital roles they will fill. As we move into the later chapters these will become clearer, but for now let me address three broad categories.

Invite. From their position inside of the church with Christian kids or from the vantage point of being on the campus on a regular basis, your leaders will have relationships that will allow them to offer an invitation to an outreach event that will be taken seriously. Show them how to do that so neither they nor the kids will feel awkward. They need to invite only the kids within their sphere of influence.

When they invite kids it is helpful to offer to pick up the kids, especially ones in junior high who do not drive. This can be viewed either as a nuisance or as a significant serving ministry. When I spoke at one church in California at a 6:30 A.M. outreach breakfast, the leaders started picking kids up at 5:30. After the breakfast they took responsibility to provide them a ride to school.

Attend. Obviously if the leaders are going to invite kids then they need to attend the event. If they bring kids with them then they need to take responsibility to make sure those kids are taken care of and are having a good time. In the process of doing that the leaders can both introduce those kids to some others they know, and/or meet the friends of the kids they brought. Both of these ministries broaden the network of personal relationships, which is at the heart of what will take place at the meeting.

HIT. No, we are not advocating abusing 9th graders. HIT stands for High Impact Teams. These are the teams that will take specific areas of responsibility for the meeting—publicity, music, set-up, and so on. (All of these details will be described in detail in chapter 9.) For now you need to understand that each of your youth leaders will be on one of these teams. The actual ministry will be carried out by the core kids, but each team will have an adult leader to guide, direct, advise and coordinate.[2]

Only with your leadership team mobilized will you be able to carry the load that will sustain a labor-intensive ministry like the outreach event. When your leaders are on your team and moving with your vision, then you will have multiplied yourself by the number of people on your team.

THE STUDENT TEAM: YOUR CRITICAL MASS

Christian students, particularly the core of kids being discipled, provide the critical mass to reach non-Christians. It makes sense. Students are with their friends six to eight hours a day, five days a week. Junior high and high school kids are the real evangelists. If they don't catch the vision of reaching their friends and act on it daily, then both campus ministry and outreach events will ultimately fail.

But I personally believe that God is raising up a generation of kids in whose hearts He is placing the desire not only to follow Him, but also to take the message of Christ to their generation. John Dawson put it this way:

The emergence of a worldwide urban culture is setting the stage for the world's first truly global awakening.... this global unification of mission fields, especially among youth, represents a significant new development...evangelists will emerge who are of junior high age.[3]

In light of the prophetic truth of that statement we need to get them on the Great Commission team. How can we do that?

Equip Kids for Evangelism. Once young people move into the discipling process, then they need the challenge to communicate their faith to others. This is not a one-dimensional, Bible-thumping approach. The process begins with friendship and goes full circle, with outreach events playing an important role in helping students show love to their friends and also express their faith. The following diagram gives the big picture of not only what's involved in kids sharing their faith, but also how outreach events fit into that.

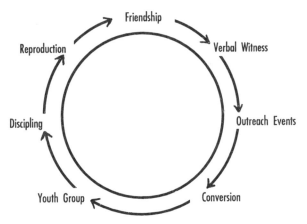

Friendship. Kids hunger for love and relationships. When Christian students radically love their friends, they earn the right to talk about their faith.

Witnessing Orally. As friendship and trust grow, a non-Christian will become receptive to an honest conversation about Jesus Christ. Encourage kids to talk about Christ early in the relationship. The big problem here is that most Christian kids have no idea how to approach the relationship or what to say when the opportunity comes.

In my own experience, with a sincere heart, and a real desire to see my friend come to Christ, I started talking to him about Christ soon after I had become a believer. He was antagonistic. I was defensive.

It ended in a shouting match. I was totally unprepared to communicate with him about Christ. All of this points out how important it is to have the proper tools to do this training effectively. Several tools are available from Reach Out Ministries to help your kids live out and articulate their faith:

Giving Away Your Faith, a 10-week discipleship course that trains students in a different aspect of witnessing each week, then has them do assignments that put what they have learned into practice.

Taking Your Campus for Christ, a book for kids on how to influence their friends by their lifestyle, prayer, and orally sharing their faith. It contains six sessions of "Dynamic Discussion Starters for Outreach to Your Friends."

The Facts of Life, a booklet for students to help them articulate the Gospel message clearly; it can also be given to the non-Christian to help him or her understand what new life in Christ is about.

Getting Started, a six-session booklet for Christians to follow up students they have led to Christ. It helps Christians get new believers established in their relationship with Christ.

Outreach Events. During the training, Christian students catch the vision for how God wants to use them and how they are to share Christ. The outreach event serves as a focal point—a place they can bring their friends, where non-Christian friends experience a Christian atmosphere and hear positively who Jesus is and how He can change a student's life.

Conversion. The outreach event serves also as a platform for ongoing conversation about Jesus Christ. At the end of the meeting, later that night, or at school the next day, the Christian student will have the opportunity to discuss the Gospel. In this kind of atmosphere, eventually the Christian student will have the opportunity to lead his friend to Christ.

Youth Group. Then the Christian student invites his newly converted friend to the youth group meeting. This provides the new believer with the opportunity to have fellowship with other Christians, to grow spiritually and to learn how to function within the body of Christ.

Discipleship. The next step is for this new believer to be discipled personally. The student who led him to Christ can take him through the *Getting Started* booklet. Then he can move into the structure of your discipleship process.

Reproduction. In the follow-up and discipleship process this new Christian will be challenged to share Christ with his non-Christian friends.

The process has come full circle. Repeated enough times by enough students, the Great Commission will be fulfilled among the young people in your community, the youth culture of America and ultimately around the world.[4]

Challenge Students to Ownership and Responsibility. This is the students' ministry, not yours. To succeed, your vision must become theirs. Most students are not challenged enough. That is why they need you to keep coming on like gangbusters with your vision and with ways they can get involved in it.

The Challenge. Many youth workers are afraid to challenge students out of fear of alienating them. You can challenge them by helping them look beyond themselves. The average junior high or high school student is bored with talking on the phone and cruising Main Street. They are bored with church, too. Check your attendance records. When they get to be juniors, they start dropping out like flies.

A teenager wants something beyond what he is experiencing right now. For you to take a student beyond himself, you must view him with an eternal perspective. That means simply seeing the student's potential—viewing him as God does. Accept him where he is, while seeing beyond that to what he can become.[5]

The Ownership. If the outreach events are staff-planned, staff-produced, staff-directed, staff-evaluated—staff, staff, staff—they won't work. Even if you put on a quality event it won't work because students will evaluate everything you do by MTV standards. When they come to your event, they will have just seen a $150-million movie a few days before. When you show them a $15 filmstrip they will sit back and say, "OK, I'll give you a D on that one."

However, when students own it, a meeting could be a D presentation, but they will give it an A because they are evaluating their peers; and they compare their peers, not with MTV, but with themselves. Even if Eric stands in front of his peers and says, "Um, er, um, I ah, um I love, um, er God," his friends will say, "Hey, dude, great talk." Why? Kids are thinking, "That's my friend up there, and he said he loved

God in front of 150 kids. That's terrific." That's one reason why student ownership is so important.

That is not to say that you don't need to have a standard of excellence. Having an attitude that "Anything done for Jesus is OK" will not cut it. It is not OK. You need to communicate to students Colossians 3:23, "Whatever you do, work at it with all your heart, as working for the Lord, not for men."

But students can do it with excellence. Work with them, not for them, to create an event that has a high standard of excellence.

The responsibility. All too often adults do not trust students with responsibility. But your ministry will multiply by the number of your core kids when you delegate responsibilities to them. By giving students responsibility you communicate, "I believe in you. I trust you." They will respond eagerly.

Allow for failure, too. They are young, often immature. Someone once said, "He who never makes mistakes, never makes anything; and he who never fails, never does anything."[6] If we expect students to grow, we need to allow them to fail. Continued trust in spite of their failures is powerful motivation.

With your visionary leadership, the leadership team gets motivated and moves into action, and your kids own the event and take responsibility, then the wave swells and rises to its crest. At that point you are prepared to let that momentum carry you into successfully creating outreach events that will make a real difference for the kingdom of God.

ACTION POINT

To assess your readiness to begin outreach events, evaluate your level of momentum right now, and then what you need to do to get totally prepared. To do that, use the "Outreach Events Readiness Assessment" on page 192 of "The Outreach Event Planner."

1. A paper entitled "Evangelism Through Youth Ministry," Rick Caldwell, 14–15.
2. The HIT team idea was taken from my church, First Baptist North in Atlanta, where Andy Stanley is the pastor.
3. John Dawson, Taking Our Cities for God, 64-66.
4. Adapted from Don Cousins, "Full-Cycle Evangelism," in *Working with Youth*, comp. Ray Willey (Wheaton, Ill.: Victor Books.)
5. Chuck Klein, "Leading and Motivating Students," in *Working with Youth*, comp. Ray Willey (Wheaton, Ill.: Victor Books.)
6. Ibid.

Six

Shout It Out: Spreading the Word

"When people think God, I want them to think about our youth ministry and our church." That is what a youth leader said to me when the school administration called him to bring his adult leaders to the school to counsel students after a suicide.

When I asked him how he got people to think about his ministry, he gave me a constant stream of creative ideas. For example, they did things like put ads in the school paper with a picture of a high school student, his favorite thing to do, his favorite song, and some other trivia, then a five- or six-sentence testimony about his relationship to Jesus. Then they would put the time and place of their outreach event inviting people to come. Then he gave me another creative example. They put a mobile sign across from the school with a message like, "Susan Hernandez knows Jesus and wants you to know him. Come to _____ at _____ to find out more." Then at their outreach event Susan would give her testimony. Every student in the school knew about their youth ministry.

He did what you want to do: *creatively spread the word in your school(s) with information about events that help students get to know Jesus Christ.*

What can we do to "shout it out" so the message is loud and clear?

CREATING A WITNESS AWARENESS

Our first responsibility is to communicate to our Christian kids that sharing Christ is something they can do. Note that the emphasis here does not revolve around the more surface issue of bringing their friends to a meeting; rather our focus is on helping them share Christ with their friends. When the time is right for this, bombard your kids with the idea that their friends need Christ and that they are God's primary tools for helping their friends know Him. To do this, use encouragement, not guilt. Concentrate on their identity in Christ, not what they *ought to* do.

Positively motivate your students to share their faith and bring their friends.

Motivate them with love and acceptance. Students will listen and follow when we meet their needs. Those needs fall into three categories.

(1) Personal needs. Every kid needs to be loved and to love others.

(2) Family needs. As we help them understand their relationships at home, deal with the pain that many of them have, and respond properly to their parents and other family members, God will bring about a dramatic change in their attitudes. That will help them to respond properly to a love relationship with God.

(3) Spiritual needs. When kids understand the following motivating truths, they will have no hesitation about sharing Christ.

- You totally accepted because of what Jesus has done for you (Ephesians 1:4-6).
- God loves you unconditionally (I John 4:10)
- You have a relationship with God that cannot be broken (John 10:27-28)
- You are as important to God as any person in the universe (Romans 5:8)
- You are a person of infinite value and worth (Psalm 139: 13-16)

When those truths have begun to sink in, then you can ask, "Wouldn't it be exciting to dream about how God could use you?" How much better than burning kids out on guilt motivation. They may talk about Christ in order to please you once or twice, but it will never be a consistent motivation without these truths as the basis.

Motivate them with grace. Let's use the definition of grace mentioned earlier. Grace is "God's supernatural ability in me through the Cross and resurrection." When kids begin to understand the resources they have in Christ, and the love and power God desires to release through them to their friends, they will have a high degree of internal motivation and confidence.

I've seen this in my son Scott. He has had a powerful, consistent witness since he was 15. That year he almost died. As a result of that trauma, he had a genuine encounter with the presence of Jesus. Since then he has never wavered in his faith. And his witness has been a challenge to me. He is the only Christian in his fraternity in college. This year, Bernie, the president, came to Scott's room one night and said, "Scott, I want you to come to my room." He told Scott how he had accepted Christ when he was in high school but had put it on the shelf while in college. Then he said, "Scott, I've been really empty for three years. I've been watching you. I know you are a follower of Christ. Would you help me get back on track with God?"

Once a kid has the motivation, I think you can do some very practical things to equip him to *share his faith and bring his friends.*

Love others. Model this in your love for them and in your love for non-Christians. As this modeling takes place through you, your leaders, and your core of discipled kids, then that will create the atmosphere in your youth group in which kids who come from the outside will feel welcome and loved. Usually this is one of the biggest hurdles to get over. How many times have I heard, "Our kids are in cliques. They won't even speak to anyone but their friends." All of these chapters of preparation will break the neck of this problem and give kids the security and freedom they have in Christ to love other people's friends who come.

Invite peers. Plan several youth group sessions that teach your kids how to relate socially. Help them develop skills such as how to remember names, how to ask good questions, and how to listen. Use role playing and skits to demonstrate how kids can do this. Have a group do it incorrectly, making someone feel awkward, embarrassed, frustrated. Then go back and do it correctly, making the person feel warm, loved, and encouraged (but not in an insincere, Eddie Haskell sort of way!). After that, show them step by step how to invite a friend.

Help them to understand that they succeed if they invite someone with love—whether that person comes or not. For most of them this means taking a real step of faith. Many of them will have to move out of their comfort zones in order to offer the invitation. Help them see that once they do it a few times, it will become a normal part of what they do every day. After you have given encouragement and instruction on this, have them practice on each other several times. Then give them the assignment to try this on one friend they have been praying for in their prayer power teams.

Be flexible and persistent. Help them to anticipate a non-Christian's response. Non-Christians will not necessarily act like the Christians they have just practiced on. Show them how to roll with the punches—to accept people where they are, regardless of their attitudes or behavior. Encourage them to keep on building the relationship and keep on inviting. Studies show that it takes seven contacts with a non-Christian before a person will respond. Remind them to invite their friends in the context on ongoing relationship, rather than a hit-and-run approach.

Identify with Jesus Christ. Your kids have to grasp that when they invite someone it is not just a "social thing," rather it is a "Jesus thing." Teach them to get the name of Jesus out in the open. Don't hide the real purpose of the event. Sure, they can talk about who will be there, and how much fun it will be, but also they can let their friends know that they will talk about Jesus.

For your kids to mention the name of Jesus probably will be their first big step toward sharing the Gospel with their friends. For some it will come easily. For others, because of temperament, personality, or where they are spiritually, it may take some time. Help them see that no matter how long it takes, it is their first big step in leading someone to Jesus.

Share the Gospel. If the conversation opens up and the person they invite expresses a real interest in Christ, then show your kids how to take the tools they have, or will learn in *Giving Away Your Faith,* and apply them in this situation—asking questions, giving their testimony, sharing the Gospel, and drawing the net.

Since we know that we can't repeat things for kids too many times, you may want to practice with them on these skills, even taking them to practice out to a place where kids hang out.

Consider carrying out this equipping process in a retreat setting. But you need to have it close to where teenagers hang out so you can go out and practice. I suggest that you use part of a weekend for this. For another approach, use your weekly youth group meetings to train them in one of these skills each week. You will know how this equipping will work best in your situation.

Once this kind of instruction is in process, then the actual publicity already has the engine running because the heart of your publicity is what the Christian kids will do with their friends. The rest of it is relatively easy.

BUILDING ROADS TO PEOPLE

Now let's construct several highways that help kids' connect to their friends.

Person to Person. They had no billboards, radios, TVs, newspapers or magazines, yet in Jesus' day "news about him spread quickly over the whole region of Galilee" (Mark 1:28). From person to person the news spread so that larger and larger crowds came to hear His message.

Today advanced technology allows us to "get the word out" more quickly, more creatively, and more powerfully than they ever could have in Jesus' day. "OK, Simon, your job is to tie into the computer bulletin board and let them know I'll feed 5,000 next Thursday at...let's see, dinner is around 6 o'clock." Can you imagine? But even with all of our high-tech toys, nothing can beat word-of-mouth publicity.

People come to meetings for a variety of reasons, but statistics show that at least 75 percent of those who come to church meetings were personally invited. To maximize the potential of this very personal approach, construct these roads to help your kids connect to their friends.

Changed lives. If the old saying is true that a picture is worth a thousand words, then a changed life is worth 10,000 fliers. When Jesus changes a student's life and his friends see that change, then they will be attracted to Jesus. The life change will create curiosity.

We see the impact of this kind of publicity in the account of the woman at the well (John 4). After Jesus had transformed her life, John says, "Many of the Samaritans from that town believed in him because of the woman's testimony" (4:39). And later "many more became believers" (v. 41). When Jesus changes a life, the word spreads rapidly. When kid's lives are changed through the witness of your kids on campus, or through your outreach event, students will know, and they will be curious.

Discipleship groups. Because of the high level of motivation and sense of accountability in your discipleship groups, you can give members the assignment to bring at least two of their non-Christian friends to the outreach event. Remember the Chuck Miller example. You will automatically have three times the number of students involved in your outreach events when this is implemented.

Youth group. Although you do not have the same level of commitment from the whole youth group as you do with the discipleship groups, you can still challenge the kids to invite their friends to the outreach event. You can motivate them by helping them see how they can influence their friends.

One of the best and most specific ways to do this is to challenge your kids to join a *prayer power team.* Then invite one person off of their list (see page 56). Another approach is to help the kids make a seating chart of one of their classes. They choose a name from the list whom they feel might be most open, and invite that person to the outreach event. (See the accompanying chart.)

JOHN	SUE	JERRY
MELISSA	**ME**	JACK
DAWN	BILL	SAM

Or you can use the prayer target to create awareness. (See page 58.)

Since kids tend to forget things, keep up the awareness level of your group. Make announcements each week using funny skits. Put up posters in all of the classrooms. Put a table in a conspicuous place with fliers and posters of coming events. Communicate to the church and the youth group using the church bulletin, the church paper, the youth group paper, and any other means possible. Don't design something different for each one, but use the same basic graphic "slick" for all of these opportunities.

Leadership team. Assign members of your leadership team a certain number of students to invite. If they minister at the schools, have them invite students from the campus. If they teach Sunday School, have them invite their kids, the fringe kids, and the students in their classes.

Structured outreach. To give all of the above ideas a formal structure you can have a structured outreach time each week. Some churches have this built into their program; others don't. You can do it before or after your youth group or on another night. You can use this in a variety of ways according to your specific situation.

Many youth workers have used the hour before the youth group or before an outreach event to mobilize students to invite their friends and to do personal evangelism. Often called "Bring 'Em Back Alive," this time slot provides students with a scheduled weekly time to share their faith and invite friends.

For this to work effectively, begin an hour and a half before the event. Have everyone meet in a designated place on time. Give them specific direction:

• Instructions: Each week remind them of their purpose in going. Give them inspiration by sharing testimonies from the week before. Offer one bibical principle and several practical tips on how to express their faith clearly. Feel free to repeat things they have heard before. Give them a few minutes to practice what they heard on each other.

• Partners: Link kids who are spiritually more mature and more skilled with younger and weaker ones. The more mature ones will have the challenge of helping the younger ones. The younger ones can learn how to express their faith better from the older ones. Also consider who they are going to see. Friends should go to see friends. This can get a little tricky, so have it well organized.

• Assignments: The teams need to know exactly who they are going to see and where they will meet them. They can go to their homes or they can meet them at some hangout or fast-food place. If they are going to a home, you need to have names, addresses, and phone numbers available either on rolodex cards or on a computer list so they can know exactly where they are going. You will need to have adult leaders who are "captains" over several teams. These adults need to be responsible to know who is on what teams, where they are going, who they are meeting. If you have younger kids who don't drive, these adults will need to be responsible to transport them. You can use church vans, church bus, or individual cars. Give them a specific time to be back.

Pray together in teams before you go. Pray for boldness in sharing and for receptive listeners.

When a team meets their friends, after a few minutes of casual conversation, the kids need to go ahead and invite their friends to the outreach event. If the opportunity presents itself share personal testimonies and the Gospel if their friends are open. Have them pray for their friends before they leave. They can ask a simple question like, "Would you mind if I prayed for you before we take off?" If the outreach event is immediately following invite them to go back to the event with you.

Telephone. We have two phone lines, and three teenagers living in our home. From 7 o'clock in the evening until at least 10 o'clock it is impossible to get a call through. Why is that? Kids fanatically, intensely, and enthusiastically use the phone!

You can take advantage of this phenomenon to publicize outreach events. Mobilize kids to do something they like to do already. In order to do this the following approach may be helpful to you.

Secure a list of the telephone numbers of students at the local high school(s). The kids in your youth group should be able to provide you with a directory.

Divide the kids who want to do this into teams. To make this experience really fun, have the teams meet at someone's home and create a party atmosphere. The teams don't need to consist of more than three people because then they won't be able to make many calls, given the fact that most homes have only one phone line.

Each team needs a leader who will take responsibility to distribute the names and to do follow up. You probably want to have your core kids or adult leaders take this responsibility.

When they arrive, assign them students to invite over the phone. Make sure they call everyone on their lists. Conduct the following telephone survey.[1] Have them personalize the conversation as much as possible. When they call, have them give their full name, and what grade they are in. Then follow with the survey. "I would like to get your opinion and advice on several questions. Would you be willing to give your responses to ten brief questions?"

Student Telephone Survey

I would like to get your opinion and advice on several questions. Would you be willing to give your response to ten brief questions?

1. Are you a member of an organized church or religious group? If yes, what denomination/group?_____

2. How often do you attend church/group services?

   ☐ More than once a week   ☐ Once a month

   ☐ Once a week   ☐ A few times a year

   ☐ Twice a month   ☐ Never

3. How often does your family engage in religious activities at home? (If needed, give an example: Bible reading, praying.)

   ☐ Very frequently   ☐ Rarely

   ☐ Often   ☐ Never

   ☐ Sometimes

4. In a sentence, what do you think the Bible is about?

   _____

5. In your opinion, who is Jesus Christ? _____

   _____

6. How much do your religious convictions influence your daily life?

   ☐ Very much

   ☐ Some

   ☐ A little

   ☐ Not at all

7. If available would you be in voluntary religious activities during school hours? (If needed, give an example: Bible study, fellowship group.)

8. If available, how interested would you be in voluntary religious activities outside of regular school hours? (If needed, give an example: outreach events, youth group.)

9. Do you believe Jesus Christ's death has anything to do with our relationship to God?

   ☐ Yes   ☐ Don't know

   ☐ No

10. Would you say that you are in control of your life or that your know Jesus Christ personally and that He is in control of your life?

    ☐ Self   ☐ Jesus

The callers can then take the conversation as far as it can go. Urge them to be bold, yet sensitive, to talk about their relationship to Christ, to allow the person on the other end to open up and share problems, and to lead the person to Christ if he or she shows that kind of interest.

At the end of the survey, if a student has shown an interest in spiritual things:

- ask that person if you could meet at school and talk some more.
- set up a time and place to meet the next day.
- get an address and phone number. Do this by offering yours first, asking for it in a friendly way, not a formal way.

COVERING THE CAMPUS

Students spend seven or more hours a day at school. Therefore it stands to reason that we want to use this forum to invite the students to outreach events.

You want to create a very positive image in the minds of the administration and the students at school. These people will perceive it either positively or negatively. For that reason it is very important for you to think through your approach.

Don't advertise what you are not, but do not play down your meeting either. Make sure that the slant you take on your publicity speaks to the needs and issues of the kids at that school. Design your publicity to communicate that—

- The outreach event is THE place to be that night.
- Kids will have fun.
- Their friends will be there.
- They will experience a first-class event.
- They will learn about Jesus Christ.

In order to accomplish these publicity objectives, you can use the following guidelines.

- Target the audience. Decide before you ever do any publicity who it is that you are trying to reach. Determine who the specific groups are within the student population and then design your publicity to reach the ones the Lord impresses you to reach. Consider groups your core kids are already in, contacts you already have with leaders of those groups, and which groups are most open to the Gospel. To do this accurately use the "School Survey" in *Penetrating the Campus*. Target your publicity to appeal to the groups you are most likely to reach. If several youth groups in your community will cooperate to do this, you will have every target group on the campus covered.

• Publicize person to person. Students' inviting their friends far exceeds the effectiveness of any other type of publicity. All of these other ideas only serve to supplement the person-to-person approach.

• Create sharp publicity. Have someone, preferably one of your students with artistic talent, design a sharp logo for your overall ministry and then unique art for each of your outreach events. Use your general youth ministry logo on every piece of publicity you produce so that students will identify your ministry with that logo.

• Follow school rules. When you consider publicizing on a school campus, you need to make absolutely sure that you do not violate any school rules. In order to do that, obtain permission beforehand. If you already have a ministry on the campus, this should not be any problem. If you do not have a ministry there, you definitely need to walk lightly. Your legal boundaries are that students can put up posters and hand out fliers on the campus, but you or your volunteers cannot. Even if you are within your legal rights, get permission so that you guard the relationship with the school.

• Consider your budget. Good publicity can be expensive, so plan your budget carefully. Find the balance between extravagance and excellence. You don't have to be extravagant to be excellent, or excellent to be extravagant. The emphasis is on *quality*. But quality doesn't necessarily mean expensive. Avoid "the cheap church stuff" syndrome. If you believe that spending a large sum of money in one area will prove effective, go for it. Just make sure the money is in the budget and that you have thought through how effective this expenditure will be.

Creatively think beyond your budget. Often local merchants who want to get their message out through advertising, and who are Christians, will work with you to do an "ad campaign" for a special event. For example, you could work together on a "bleacher seat" for athletic events. On one side, the merchant advertises his or her business, on the other side you advertise your event(s). But be careful that a beer logo doesn't show up on the item somewhere!

Focus your approach. Limit the number of ideas you try. As you filter through the proposed ideas, take two or three of the best ones and use those instead of trying to do them all. Once you have tried two or three, add in another one, or substitute one for variety's sake. This is only a sampling of ideas. The truth is that, from your creative times of brainstorming, you, your leaders and your students will come up with much better ideas than these. You can use some of the following ideas or come up with your own.

• Posters. Depending on the event, you can create your own (just like the cheerleaders do) or use a "professional" poster—either one that you get done at a printer or you get from the group that is coming in for your event. Either way you go on this is fine. When you create your own, it is labor intensive. My daughter Katie was a cheerleader. The number of hours she spent working on creative posters was astronomical. You will need a team in your youth group who does this kind of thing well.

• Tracts. As one creative option, print a personalized tract. Use photographs of four Christian kids on the campus, along with a brief testimony from each one. You can use the back page for a brief Gospel presentation, but you want to keep the reader guessing also. Use one section of it to announce your event. You can print something like this for less than you can buy one from the bookstore. Consider having several versions with a variety of kids' testimonies. Because of its personalized nature, your students will not be shy about passing it around.

• School newspapers. Many junior and senior high schools publish a school newspaper. Merchants or any other group that wishes to pay can advertise in these publications. For a small amount of money you can advertise your outreach event. You can use the testimony idea here as well. If it will help your budget, you can get one of the businessmen in your church to underwrite this and then use that company's name in the ad. In putting the ad together, work with a professional printer so that the message you want to communicate comes across clearly.

• Public address announcements. If someone in your youth group (like a student government leader) has access to the school announcements, that person can announce the event. The boundaries are that this needs to be done by a student, and without singling out a specific church. Keep it generic and neutral. You can try another angle on this by having the announcement made at the school sports events—both varsity and junior varsity. Usually schools have someone who announces the games. Make certain that whoever writes the announcement gets your approval on it since your reputation is on the line at the school.

• Fliers. Put together a 4" x 6" or 5" x 8" flier announcing the event. Give it to your youth group to hand out at school. On the day of the meeting have students give them to people at school and personally invite those people to attend. Make sure that your kids do not trash the school with these fliers. In order to maintain your positive image with the school, it is imperative that someone take responsibility to pick up the discarded fliers after school. You can work with the custodian on this.

• Mailings. Sending out information and invitations to your outreach event through mailings creates a general awareness of your event. Never count on it to bring anyone specifically to the event. It won't. However it will inform. It does create an image. And it opens the door for you and your students to invite people to the event.

In the course of the school year your goal could be to do at least one mailing to the entire student body. You will have to determine if and how you can do this according to your budget. The use of mailings has a variety of applications.

You can send a mailing every week. If you have a weekly outreach event and a large budget, this is a good option. You can mail information every month with a sharp presentation of all that is happening during the month. You can mail to sections of the student body, spreading the mailings out so that a certain number get invited each week. That not only spreads out your expenses, but also piques the interest of other students who have not gotten anything in the mail.

Create your own strategy for how you can use this idea the best for your unique situation.

• Special group invitations. Invite different groups, clubs, and school organizations to come to the outreach event. If you do a weekly event, you can invite different groups to come on different weeks. For example,

89

you can invite the drama team one week and the track team the next. Schedule these at least a month ahead of time so that the group can get the event on its schedule, promote it within the group, and plan on how it will handle transportation. All of this will ensure a larger representation.

To make certain that the situation is handled without communication breakdowns, give the responsibility to serve as a liaison to a student in your church who is a part of that group. One extension of this idea is to have one student or a team of two students who are in a club or organization at school take that group on as their responsibility. The goal wold be to get members of the group to come as a group to every outreach event.

• Advertisements. This covers a wide variety of publicity options that will allow you and your students to use creativity to communicate an awareness about your outreach events.

Trailer signs. Rent trailer signs and place them strategically across the street in front of the school. Put slogans on the signs using the names of your strong Christian kids. For example, one youth minister had a girl in his group named Donna Eagle. He designed the sign to read: "Donna Eagle Goes to NiteLife. She's No Turkey." Obviously you will want to get the student's permission before you do this! In your youth group have a contest to come up with the most clever slogans to put on the sign.

Book covers. Before the school year begins, design a book cover that your students can use that tells the events you have coming up during the school year. Put the time, place, and any other useful information on these covers. Do not include any information that will go out of date quickly. The book cover should include your logo. Your youth group can work on this as a project during the summer. After they get the information, then take it to a graphic designer and a professional printer to get it completed in an excellent manner.

T-shirts. Put your logo and the event on a T-shirt design. Include the time and place.

Buttons. Like the book covers and T-shirts, you can advertise your event with buttons. But with buttons you can do it less expensively. Ask your kids to wear them on the day of, or week of, your outreach event.

Community Advertisements. Students hang out in many different places and get their messages from numerous sources. That is why you will find it so important to advertise in the general community, focusing on those places where kids get their messages, such as fast food restaurants, rec centers, cruising strips, skating rinks, pools, beaches, and malls. One team of students can take on the responsibility to hand out fliers and put up posters in these places.

Local newspapers. Depending on the size of your community and the newspaper's policies, you can place articles and/or pictures in the local newspaper about a community-wide event. Write your own press release; then invite the religion editor or a writer from the paper to interview you and some of your students. Better yet, invite the reporter to the event. When you place an ad, design it yourself. If you put one in once a month or on four consecutive weeks leading up to a big event, then you will need to design several that will provide variety. Ask them to put it in the sports section, not stuck in some section of the paper that no one reads. In a smaller paper with more personal contacts, you have a better opportunity to place regular articles and ads. At a larger paper you compete more for space. Plan your approach accordingly. Check the cost on all of this and reconcile it with your budget.

Radio and television. Use public service time to announce upcoming events. Write your announcement, then call it in to the local radio and television station. To put a creative touch to this, have your kids write the announcement and then record it. You can do the same for TV if you have the equipment and kids who can do some acting. Try another angle on this by getting you and your kids on local talk shows to talk about the upcoming event. Or if you are having a guest speaker or artist, have the station do an interview with him or her, either by phone for radio, or on a TV show on the day before or day of the event. If you have a contact at the radio or TV station, that person can help you know exactly how to approach this best in your situation.

GATHERING NEEDED RESOURCES

In order to assist you to do your outreach with excellence and quality, I have included several resources that you may want to use. Many of them are available directly from Reach Out Ministries.

Sharing Christ
Giving Away Your Faith, Barry St. Clair (Victor Books)

Taking Your Campus for Christ, Barry St. Clair (Victor Books)

Building love and unity
Up Close and Personal, Wayne Rice, Youth Specialties, 1224 Greenfield Dr., El Cajon, CA 92021. 1-800-776-8008. A 13-week curriculum that helps build closeness and resolve conflict.

Relating socially
Getting Kids to Mix, Len Woods (Victor Books)

Serious Fun and *More Serious Fun,* Dave Veerman (Victor Books)

"Community Building," *Youth Worker Journal* (Fall 1993), 1224 Greenfield Dr., El Cajon, CA 92021.

Targeting your audience
Penetrating the Campus, Barry St. Clair and Keith Naylor (Victor Books)

"The Target," Student Discipleship Ministries, P.O. Box 6747, Ft. Worth, TX 76115.

Creating art work
The Youth Specialties Clip Art Book, vols. 1 and 2, 1224 Greenfield Drive, El Cajon, CA 92021, 1-800-776-8008.

"Youth Workers' Promo Kit," The Church Art Works, 875 High St. NE, Salem, OR 97301.

"ArtSource," vols. 1–6, The Church Art Works, 875 High St. NE, Salem, OR 97301, or order from Youth Specialties at 1-800-776-8008.

Creating announcements with skits
Skits, vols. 1 and 2, Young Life, P.O. Box 520, Colorado Springs, CO 80901.

Writing for the newspaper, radio, and TV
"How to Beat Media Phobia," Julia Duin, *Ministries Today* (March/April 1992): 55–61. For a copy of this excellent article, contact *Ministries Today* at 407-333-0600.

Also see the sample press release in "The Outreach Event Planner" on page 195.

ACTION POINTS

Out of all that has been presented to help you "shout it out," you need to design your own personalized strategy to fit your own unique situation. Try to plan it out for a whole budget year. Use "The Outreach Event Planner," on page 193-194, then check here when you have completed your publicity plan.

☐ Publicity Plan completed.

---

1. Survey contributed by John Musselmann, formerly youth pastor at Coral Ridge Presbyterian Church, Ft. Lauderdale, Florida, and now the director of The Jackson Institute in Atlanta, Georgia.

Seven

Deliver the Knock-Out Punch, Part 1: Planning the Program

Right in the middle of the "cruising zone," on a mall parking lot, they set up for a Saturday night outreach. Even before the band began to play, over 100 kids gathered around, just because they saw people unloading sound equipment.

As the band began to play, about 250 people crowded around. The vast majority of them smoking, drinking non-believers. The band from the church played very contemporary music for twenty minutes, then the leader gave a clear expression of his conversion and commitment to Jesus Christ. Many of the kids gathered knew him from his days as a leader while in high school and his involvement in a rock group. They listened intently to his powerful but non-threatening presentation.

Just before the intermission the band announced it would come back in fifteen minutes to play again. Then they told the crowd that during the break each person would have the opportunity to talk to someone about their relationship to Jesus Christ. As soon as the break began, the trained young people from the church turned to the people around them to talk about Jesus.

By the close of the evening, nine people had prayed to receive Christ. A counseling area behind the sound equipment truck had been set up, where these and others talked further.[1]

We can use the description of this unique outreach event to stimulate our thinking about how we put together the program for our events, whether they occur on an occasional or a regular basis. Several very important lessons will guide our overall thinking.

Center on evangelism. The clear purpose of the above event was to reach kids with the gospel of Christ, not to entertain. For that event 100 kids with a burden to reach their friends received training to mix with the crowd, build a relationship, and share the message of Christ. Even though the sharing was direct, no one was pressured to talk about Christ.

Use variety. Avoid locking into one format. Obviously the above format would not be used on a weekly basis. You will discover that with the ingredients in the next two chapters you will have an almost infinite variety of options for both weekly and one-time events. Be creative. Keep them guessing. Use the element of surprise.

Prepare properly. For a week the leaders had worked on the details of the program. Earlier in the evening 100 kids met for prayer and a thorough explanation of what would happen at the event. Everyone knew where to be and what to do. All details were tended to, such as taking proper security measures and making necessary legal arrangements.

Follow up. Each person who attended was important. All were engaged in conversation at the end with a specific question about the event. Those who did not make a decision were challenged to keep thinking and their friends were prepared to ask them further questions. Those who made a decision had a friend assigned to get with them the next day to help them get started in following Christ. Because of that, almost all of those nine students got involved in the church.

To put together the program for an outreach event like this, what do we do?

GETTING YOUR DUCKS IN A ROW[2]

No matter what size our church, our budget, or our resources, every one can program an effective outreach event by implementing seven steps of development.

(1) Purpose. In your meeting, you can't do everything. So narrow your purpose. Later in this chapter and in chapter 8, we will see all of the options for a program. You will have many more than you can use in one event. If you know your specific purpose for that event,

you will be able to choose the right ingredients to make your program work properly.

You can determine your purpose by considering these three questions:

- Where does this event fit into the strategy/vision/mission of our youth ministry?
- What is going on in the youth culture, particularly what is God desiring to say to the kids in our community right now?
- Where does this event fit into the calendar year?

Then write out your specific purpose for this event.

(2) *Target.* The old saying is true: "If you aim at nothing, you will hit it every time." In light of that, you need to determine who your target audience is. You may say: "Kids!" Great. What kids?

You can determine the specific answer to that by answering these questions:

- Who will be in the audience?
- Where do they stand spiritually?
- What are their needs?
- How old are they?
- Where are they developmentally?

Then write out specifically who your audience will be.

(3) *Theme.* "Don't cast your message to the wind, rather let the wind catch your message." In other words, don't just pick some theme out of the air. Instead *focus* your theme. In prayer ask the Holy Spirit to show you exactly what the kids who come will need to experience.

You can decide what the overall thrust of your theme should be by answering these questions:

- What does the Holy Spirit seem to be saying?
- What do the students who are coming need to hear?
- What will meet a specific, focused need?
- What will have spiritual authenticity?

Write down what your theme will be.

(4) *Goal.* Within the general theme, we need to ask, "What is our *one* goal?" That goal should target an emotion, a feeling. When that has been decided, then you will have narrowed your focus to the degree

that you can enable your audience to understand, and you can help convince them to respond.

You can come to that goal by asking yourself these questions:

- What emotion/feeling do we want to target?
- What is our rationale for communicating that emotion/feeling?
- What is the one thing we want to say about that emotion/feeling?

Write out your specific goal in one sentence.

(5) Ideas. Now we want to put flesh on the bones. What are the ideas you can use to communicate your goal? To come up with these ideas, rely on a team of people. Brainstorm. One person's ideas are not enough. No idea is a bad idea. Encourage creativity. Ask the Holy Spirit to give you the right ideas.

You will have more ideas than you can use if you ask yourself these questions:

- What have we seen at the mall that relates to our goal?
- What have we read in kids' magazines that relates to the goal?
- What drives do kids have that relate to the goal?
- What are we seeing on TV/commercials/MTV that relates to the goal?

Write down your ideas related to your theme and goal.

(6) Resources. Quality and depth come with the resources, but those resources need to be cultivated and created. People, musical talent, trained leaders, student disciples, videos, drama talent, speakers, counsellors: all of these are resources that can enhance your event. In your situation you may have limited or vast resources available to you. Either way, determine what they are; then figure out ways to broaden and expand your resources. Each time you plan an outreach event you will need to call on some or all of your resources. Determine what you need for each event.

You will have a realistic assessment of your resources if you answer these questions:

- What resources do I have presently?
- What resources do I need that I don't have?
- How can I secure the resources I need, but don't have?

Write down the resources you need for this particular event.

(7) Production. Now it is time to put all of the pieces together. At this point the program director (probably that's you) or a small program task team will need to look at the big picture and bring it all together.

To do that you will want to use the Program Flow Chart in "The Outreach Event Planner" on page 197. Taking this approach forces you to plan ahead. You should be going through this process about one month before your event. An event that happens every week makes the planning process more intense.

When all the questions above are answered succinctly, you will have the outline of your program. (Use "The Outreach Planner" on page 196 to answer the questions for each of these seven steps and for an ongoing guide to plan your program.)

Going through this process, as time consuming as it is, will produce a program of excellence and quality in order that "God may open to us a door for the Word, so that we may speak forth the mystery of Christ" (Col. 4:3).

CREATE THE RIGHT ENVIRONMENT

How many times have you heard people say, "When I walked in the room I could feel something special." You want kids making the kinds of statements that were made in one outreach-oriented youth group.

"I sensed love. People came up to me that I didn't know and began to talk to me. I even saw a girl that I used to do drugs with. She came over and hugged me. She seemed really different." (A 17-year-old runaway)

"It felt good at first. Kinda felt at ease by the welcome I received and the fun music, but then things began to get serious and I felt funny. It was heavy, like God was speaking to me inside." (A 15-year-old boy who had never been in church before)

"I feel loved here, accepted, safe. Things are pretty bad around my house." (A senior abused by a parent)

"Right in the middle [of the meeting] I began to realize I didn't have Christ in my heart. I've been counting on my church membership to get me to heaven, but the more I was around the kids in the youth group I began to notice something missing in my life." (A girl who accepted Christ right after the meeting)[3]

I've spoken at events with elaborate facilities and all the high-tech "stuff," and the environment felt as cold as ice. On the other hand, I've spoken in some "barns" where the place was electric with excitement. What made the difference? Just like lamps, plants, and pictures in a room give it warmth, certain essential, well-placed decorations create the kind of warm atmosphere that draws students. Assuming that you have applied the earlier chapters that are so essential to creating the right atmosphere, place these five intangible, but essential, decorations to create atmosphere.

Compassion. Kids can "feel" whether they are being loved or not. And most of them don't feel they are. In an ABC News survey of thousands of students, 90 percent could not answer "Yes" to the statement "I have at least one person who I am convinced really loves me." If we love and accept them—no matter what they think, say, do or believe—the feeling of caring, openness, and friendliness will prevail.

A car cannot be towed out of the mud without someone going to it, hitching it to another vehicle, and pulling; and students cannot be led out of spiritual mud if you do not go to them, find the common link, and pull. Touching their lives with compassion provides that link.

That kind of "loving link" won't just happen. You can structure it so that every kid who shows up has a friend. Make sure that

- Adult leaders invite kids they know from the campus or church, and then take responsibility to introduce them to others at the meeting.

- Discipled kids bring at least two friends each. At the meeting they stick with them like glue, making sure they get introduced to other kids they may not know.

- The program includes interaction that allows for relaxed relationships. Crowd-breakers, mixers, and fun songs create this relaxed feel.

- Kids who come are prayed for so that they will sense God's Spirit.

Communication. When a student comes to a "religious" event for the first time, he probably expects to be bored, or scared that someone will handle snakes, or that someone will do something weird like hang from the chandeliers. He will have his guard up until he feels comfortable.

Therefore we need to communicate to secular kids right where they are. That takes effort. Work hard at eliminating the "churchy" things that cause non-Christians to feel uncomfortable and turned off. Add elements that awaken their imagination and interest without compromising your convictions. You can do that by asking yourself these questions:

- What behavior or practices can we identify that might turn off secular students?

- What can we put in the place of the things that turn them off?

Place the plants of communication throughout the program.

Connections. You can stage phenomenal programs, but you can't compete with what Hollywood can put in their hand for $9.99. They can stick in a video for that amount or less any time and beat your most extravagant effort. The program is not your connection into that secular kid's life. *Relationships are.* If a student comes on the basis of an entertaining program, then the first time he doesn't like it he won't come back. But if he comes on the basis of a relationship, he will keep coming back because of that relationship.

To build a vast network of these connections, challenge your core kids to bring their friends.

- Give them the specific challenge to bring the kids they are praying for in their prayer power team.

- Encourage them to take these friends home afterwards and discuss the topic focused on at the event.

- When a non-Christian expresses an interest in knowing Christ, resist the temptation to lead that student to Christ. Allow the student who brought him to do that.

- Assign the follow-up responsibility for the new Christian to the student who led him to Christ.

All of these steps builds a natural bridge between the campus and the church, between the secular student and fellowship in the body of Christ.

Hang the pictures of relationships all around the room of your outreach program.

Creativity. Most people don't view themselves as very creative. However, if the creative God created you, and the creative Holy Spirit lives inside of you, then, even if you don't have natural creativity, you can call on the supernatural creativity God has put inside of you. *You are creative. Tap into it.*

To get you started creatively use the following ideas.

Provide a time of rowdiness. Kids have mega-energy. Allow them to release it at the meeting. You can channel it into a competition time, crowd-breakers, mixers, or music.

"Salt" students. That means that you create in them a thirst to hear and respond to what will be communicated in the message later in the meeting. Students need to hear the message, but before they will listen receptively and respond, they must sense the need for what is being offered. Jesus created a desire in the Samaritan woman by expressing his own need for a drink, by asking her penetrating questions and by telling her how many husbands she had (John 4). Using films, skits, dramas, testimonies and any other creative means you can think of, you can create this thirst in students. It will happen most effectively when you address their felt needs.

Involve students. As you plan the program, plan as much student participation as possible. Put students up front. Use a student emcee or emcees so they can play off of each other in making announcements and moving the program along. Kids love to see their friends up front, and they like the "hands on" involvement when you program for their participation.

Scatter the knick-knacks of your creativity all over the place.

Content. Most students either do not know or cannot articulate their real needs. But they can readily identify their felt needs—dating, sex, friends, parents, self-esteem, popularity, peer pressure, and so on. Through their felt needs you will be able to get to their real needs for faith, hope, love through Jesus Christ.

Base your content on the Bible. Students need to know that the Bible relates to their felt needs as well as to their real needs. They are fascinated when they see that the Bible relates to who they are and how they live. If we appeal to the 3 E's—emotions, entertainment, and experience—then it becomes easy to manipulate students. The church has done that to kids in the past to gain quick converts. It's so sad to see kids come so close to the truth, only to walk away without it. When they are manipulated into a decision, they can't be found three days later. Kids eventually see through it and resent it. They want you to address their problems and issues, help them see bibical solutions, and put it in their language. When you do, they will hang on every word.

Put down the rug of God's Word in your program. When you decorate the room with these "essential intangibles" you will create the kind of atmosphere that will draw kids to Christ in a way that they will not be able to explain. They will come again and again because you have created something special that makes them feel loved, accepted and safe. What a great atmosphere to meet Jesus Christ!

STRUCTURE THE MEETING

You have an hour to an hour and fifteen minutes to accomplish your goals in your outreach event. It is impossible to cram every element into each event. Therefore you have to choose carefully which elements will move you toward your goal for the event. In no way can we exhaust the potential resources in this book. The following ideas are only "starters" to stir your creative juices and to provide resources.

Crowd-breakers. To break the ice, expend energy, release tension and enhance relationship building, the crowd-breaker is an excellent device. Designed for fun, the crowd-breaker can disarm fearful, tense or skeptical students quickly.

Resources:

- *Getting Kids to Mix,* Len Woods, Victor Books, 1825 College Avenue, Wheaton, IL 60187.

- *Ideas,* vols. 1–52, Youth Specialties, 1224 Greenfield Dr., El Cajon, CA 92021. 1-800-776-8008. Cited as the number one youth group resource in America, these books will have more crowd-breakers and mixers than you can ever use. Be sure to order the "Ideas Index" so you can access the information easily.

- *Youth Ministry Encyclopedia,* Lyman Coleman, Serendipity House, Box 1012, Littleton, CO 80160.

Games and Competition. Like crowd-breakers, games build energy and enthusiasm. Maximize the effect with competition. Compete between grades if you have only one school represented, or compete between schools if you have several represented.

Games and competition can develop a sense of team spirit, unity, and belonging for individual students. Once the teams are divided, have each of them choose a name, a color, and a cheer. Award competition points for this. If you do an outreach event on a regular basis, organize one or two competitive games over the next four to eight weeks. Announce the scores each week. At the end the winning team receives an award such as free ice cream or a scholarship to camp.

You will need to choose and create balance between two types of games: observation games and participation games. Observation games involve only a few people while everyone else watches. For example, an old standby is "The Cracker Eating Contest." Call a representative from each grade or school to the stage. Each one eats a pack of crackers, then drinks a soft drink to wash it down. The winner is the first one who can eat the crackers and whistle.

Participation games, on the other hand, involve everyone in semiathletic competition. Ample space and high ceilings are needed for most of these games. They work best in a warehouse or gym. When weather permits and it fits your goals, you can play outdoor games. An example of a participation game is "Knock Your Bag Off." Each person has a paper bag that fits over his head and a few pages of a newspaper rolled up as a "whacker." Divided into two or more teams, the players try to knock the opposing team members' bags off their heads without losing their own bag. The team that knocks all of the other team's bags off first wins.

Encourage your core kids and leadership to jump into this with great enthusiasm to draw in the reticent, "too cool" skeptics. Be careful that this does not get out of hand, especially with the guys getting too "into it." Don't emphasize athletic skill, but rather participation. You will have to work hard to find a balance doing games that will challenge the more athletically inclined while being interesting enough to attract the kids who couldn't care less about any kind of competition.

Resources:

- *The New Fun Encyclopedia,* vol. 1, "Games." Revised by Bob Sessoms, Abingdon Press. 201 8th Ave. S., Nashville, TN 37202. 615-749-6145.

- *Compact Encylopedia of Games,* Mary Hohenstein, Bethany House, Minneapolis, MN 55438.

- *Junior High Game Nights* and *More Junior High Game Nights*, Dan McCollam and Keith Betts, Youth Specialties, 1224 Greenfield Dr., El Cajon, CA 92021. 1-800-776-8008. Wild and crazy outreach events for junior high.

- *Play It* and *Play It Again*, Wayne Rice and Mike Yaconelli, Youth Specialties, 1224 Greenfield Dr., El Cajon, CA 92021. 1-800-776-8008.

- *Great Games for City Kids*, Nelson E. Copeland, Jr., Youth Specialties, 1224 Greenfield Dr., El Cajon, CA 92021. 1-800-776-8008. Over 200 games for urban youth.

- *Adventure Games*, Jeff Hopper, Steve Torrey, and Rod Yonkers, Youth Specialties, 1224 Greenfield Dr., El Cajon, CA 92021. 1-800-776-8008.

Skits. Fun summarizes in one word what skits do for an outreach event. Like crowd-breakers and games, they are high energy. Even though they are for fun, if you do your research you can find skits that communicate the theme of the event.

Depending on your theme and goal, you have several options as to the kinds of skits you use—reading, scripted, no script, or ad lib. Preview the skit beforehand in order to time it and check out its content. A skit that is too long or creates an embarrassing situation can dull the sharp edge of your event. Plan carefully here.

Resources:

- *The Greatest Skits on Earth*, vols. 1 and 2, Wayne Rice and Mike Yaconelli, Youth Specialties, 1224 Greenfield Dr., El Cajon, CA 92021. 1-800-776-8008. Volume 1 contains only fun skits. Volume 2 features skits with a message.

- *Skits*, vols. 1 and 2, Young Life, P.O. Box 520, Colorado Springs, CO. 80901.

Announcements. To publicize other activities for students you need to make announcements. Use them to inform your kids and to draw kids on the fringe into other areas of your church's youth ministry.

If they are presented haphazardly, in large numbers, and all in the same read-it-off-the-sheet style, then announcements become numbing, boring, and quickly forgotten. Carefully-selected and properly-prepared announcements, using creativity and humor, will present fun, clear information about future events.

To ensure that students do not forget the announcements, you can use some creative options.

Skits. Use a skit from one of the resources, or have students creatively write their own skits. For example, if you are having a swimming/water skiing event, design a skit in which students come into the meeting outfitted in water skis and canoes.

Puppets. Every age loves puppets. When puppets speak cleverly and clearly, students listen. Make sure to design the announcement so that the students remember the announcement, not just the puppets.

Newscasts. Create an announcement in which two students act like a news anchor team. Show slides behind them to highlight the message and provide humor. Mix spoof stories about people in your audience into the announcements.

Talk shows/TV shows. Students design the announcements around a talk show, soap opera, or sitcom format.

Songs. Write a song about the upcoming event and have some students sing it, preferably ones who cannot sing well.

Characters. Create a character who will give the same announcement several weeks in a row. He comes barging into the meeting several weeks in advance looking for the bus to camp, for instance. He has his suitcase, sleeping bag, inner tube, one ski, and bunches of clothes. He has on his body everything needed for camp. And he wants to go right now. Someone interviews him every week for the next several weeks about camp. His enthusiasm builds every week, and more students are involved with him in this as the weeks progress.

Resources:

- Use the resources from the skits section to help with announcements.
- Having your skit team make up their own skits is usually more creative, unique and fun than anything else.
- Puppets—contact the One-Way Street Puppet Co., P.O. Box 2898, Littleton, CO 80161.

Dramas. Moving from the fun to the serious, drama can introduce the theme of the meeting and provide an excellent means to "salt" the students. Often drama becomes your most powerful tool of communication.

To do drama well you will need someone with experience to lead the drama team, and kids with some degree of talent and/or experience.

If a drama is poorly performed, it will have little or no effect, and can even take away from positive communication. When you do it, do it well.

Resources:

- *Ideas*, especially vols. 17–20, edited by Wayne Rice, Youth Specialties, 1224 Greenfield Dr., El Cajon, CA 92021. 1-800-776-8008.

- Paul and Nicole Johnson, "God's Word Brought to Life," 254 Glenstone Circle, Brentwood, TN 37027-3917. 615-377-0093.

- Lillenas Publishing Co., P.O. Box 527, Kansas City, MO 64141.

- National Drama Service, Baptist Sunday School Board, 127 Ninth Ave. N., Nashville, TN 37234.

- One-Way Street Puppet Co., P.O. Box 2898, Littleton, CO 80161.

- *Option Plays*, Chap Clark, Duffy Robbins, and Mike Yaconelli, *Tension Getters, Tension Getters Two, Amazing Tension Getters*, David Lynn and Mike Yaconelli, Youth Specialties, 1224 Greenfield Dr., El Cajon, CA 92021. 1-800-776-8008. These real-life problems and predicaments dramatize the issues kids face and open the door for lively discussions about them.

- *Super Sketches for Youth Ministry*, Debra Poling and Sharon Sherbondy, Youth Specialties, 1224 Greenfield Dr., El Cajon, CA 92021. 1-800-776-8008. From Willow Creek Community Church, these sketches illustrate the real life issues and struggles kids face.

Visual Media. Video, slides, films, and other visual media not only "salt" students for the message to come, but can pack a powerful wallop by themselves. The key here is selecting film, video, slides, sections from cartoons and movies that carefully communicate the event's theme.

To maximize the use of visual media consider these approaches.

Create your own slide presentation or video. Kids talented in this area can take pictures on campus, interview students around the theme for the event, edit the slides or video, and then put some contemporary music behind it that also communicates the theme.

Kids like nothing more than seeing their faces or their friends' faces on the screen. Remind the visual media team to film a variety of students, not just the Christians, the popular ones or the leaders.

Create announcements using slides or video. To create interest in upcoming events—camp, a retreat, a seminar or other activity—film the previous event. Using about ten rolls of film and a 35-millimeter camera or a video camera, take a variety of action shots of kids in both fun and serious situations. After the event, edit it and show it to the kids, then put it away to use to promote the same event next time it comes around. For these kinds of high-energy, fast-paced productions, you will need to plan ahead to include them in your budget.

Show clips from old shows or movies. To enhance communication about the theme, take a scene from a secular film, TV show, or cartoon that illustrates your theme. Clips from old TV shows like "The Andy Griffith Show" or "Leave It to Beaver" are hilarious. The possibilities here are endless. Keep the clip in the four- to seven-minute range, then bring the speaker on immediately after the clip.

Show a full-length film, a video series, or multimedia show. Obviously, if you use this approach, it will take your entire program. That is fine if it communicates your theme. Make sure that the message you want to communicate is clear. Always preview the material beforehand. Often this approach lends itself to a lively discussion afterward. Be sure to have prepared the exact questions to discuss. Write them out clearly beforehand. If appropriate, give a challenge at the end of the presentation.

Music video. Armed with the latest comtemporary music videos you can do some serious damage in communicating topics and themes. Kids love these. Just make sure you don't overuse this form of communication.

Resources:

Order catalogues and keep them on file for future planning. In the appendix you will find other media resources of major film companies.

- Mars Hill Productions, 12705 S. Kirkwood, #218, Stafford, TX 77477. 1-800-580-6479. Their award-winning short and medium length films are geared for youth outreach.

- Media International, 313 E. Broadway, Suite 202, Glendale, CA 91209. 818-242-5314.

- Motivational Media, 148 South Victory, Burbank, CA 91502. 818-848-1980. These multimedia presentations express bibical truth to secular audiences on subjects such as substance abuse, racial conflict, and other significant issues.

- Camfel Productions, 15709 Arrow Highway, Suite #2, Irwindale, CA 91706. 818-960-6922. Camfel offers a variety of multimedia productions and short sports films. Special versions for large assemblies are shown in thousands of high schools annually. Sponsor one film in a school during the day, then invite the students to an outreach event that night.

- Paragon Productions, Campus Crusade for Christ, 13232 Old Meridian St., Carmel, IN 46032. 317-571-2077. The purpose and scope of Paragon is similar to that of Camfel.

- Power Surge Video Media International, 313 E. Broadway, #202, Glendale, CA 91209. 818-242-5314. Offers excellent issues-oriented youth videos.

- Translight Media Associates, 1900 Hicks Rd., Rolling Meadows, IL 60008. 708-690-7780. Offers three- to five-minute presentations that use visual images (photography).

- AMC-American Movie Classics, 150 Crossways Park West, Woodbury, NY 11797. 516-364-2222. Order old movies from this company.

- Edge TV, 1-800-366-7788. This company's videos deal with issues kids face straight on. They are designed to stimulate discussion.

- Fire by Night, P.O. Box 606, Colorado Springs, CO 80901-0606. 719-593-0444. Dramatic, comedy, and music videos for students.

- Gospel Films, P.O. Box 455, Muskegon, MI 49443. 1-800-253-0413 or 616-773-3361. Offers a wide range of outreach films for young people.

- Interl'inc, 5295 Crown Drive, Franklin, TN 37064. 615-790-9080. Video and audio music tapes with Bible studies and discussion starters.

- TWENTYONEHUNDRED Productions, 6400 Schroeder Rd., Madison, WI 53711. 608-274-9001. This ministry of InterVarsity offers innovative multimedia tools for ministry. Aimed primarily at the college/university audience, these productions stimulate discussion and help students confront issues.

- Visual Parables of Multi-Media Celebrations, c/o Edward McNulty, Northminster Presbyterian Church, 301 Forest Ave., Dayton, OH 45405. 513-222-1171. Over 30 multimedia productions aimed at young people, plus a media newsletter and training.

Testimonies. When kids stand in front of their peers and tell about their relationship to Jesus Christ and how God is working in their lives, it's always HOT! Testimonies bring Christ from the abstract to the concrete, from principles to a personal level. Spiritual power is released at an eye to eye, peer to peer level.

In order for students to express Christ well, they need to prepare well. To help them prepare, follow these suggestions.

Watch closely. Stay tuned in to which kids receive Christ and which ones are experiencing life change. Pick out kids whose lives are changing in the same area as the theme for the event.

Select carefully. Nothing will harm the witness of the youth ministry more than putting a compromising student in front of the meeting, especially if the other students look up to him. Check out his consistency and dedication by asking the student and several of his friends how he is doing with the Lord. Put a student up front because Jesus is changing his life, not because he is a good speaker, popular or funny.

Share briefly. When you invite a student to share a testimony, and when you introduce him at the meeting, ask him to share briefly. Give him a time limit and help him prepare to remain within that time limit.

Write concisely. Using the outline and suggestions in *Giving Away Your Faith,* help him write out his testimony several days in advance. Go over it with him several times. Help him stay within two to three minutes.

Speak freely. Kids will come into this nervous, ill-prepared, and inexperienced. But it is their ministry and it needs to rise and fall on them. When they finish, no matter how they do, find some positive comments to make about their presentation. Help them work through how they can improve.

Use variety. So you will not become predictable, use various types of testimonies.

- The three minute. Discussed above.

- The one sentence. Numerous students pop up and say, "Jesus is changing me in my relationship to . . . (parents, boyfriend, etc.).

- The finish-the-phrase. Several students complete the sentence, "I know I am a Christian because . . ." or other sentence completions that would relate to the theme.

- The prayer request. Students stand and say, "I need prayer for...."

- The confession. Students say, "Help me, God, as I struggle with...."

- The thanks. Students say, "I thank God for...."

- The praise. Students say, "I praise God for...."

- The small group. Preassign groups and have your discipleship group kids give a testimony about what God is doing in their lives.

Because students can identify with each other's struggles and stories, non-Christian kids will see in the testimonies of the Christians how it really is possible for them to become followers of Jesus.

Resources:

- *Giving Away Your Faith,* Barry St. Clair, Victor Books. 1-800-473-9456. This book devotes an entire chapter to helping students prepare their testimonies.

We'll pick up the rest of the outreach event elements as we continue in the next chapter.

ACTION POINT

1. Work through "Getting Your Ducks in a Row," the Program Flow Chart and the Environment Evaluation in "The Outreach Event Planner" on page 196–198.

2. Gather all of the resources listed in this chapter that you have in your library already. Decide what resources you have to have now, and figure out where you will get the money to pay for them. Decide which ones can wait and how you will budget to get them in the next 12 months.

1. This story was given to me by Rick Caldwell and occured as an outreach of his church.
2. The material under this heading was adapted from Bo Boshears, Student Impact, Willow Creek Community Church, South Barrington, Illinois. Used with permission.
3. Quotes from kids who come to Rick Caldwell's outreach events.

Eight

Deliver the Knock-Out Punch, Part 2: Carrying Out the Program

The building had 800 kids jammed into it. The room felt electric with energy and excitement. As the guest speaker, I had only one responsibility, so I sat back and watched how the meeting unfolded. Stuart, the youth pastor, was only a year or two out of college, but I could see he knew what he was doing. Prayer had permeated the preparation. All that I described in the publicity chapter he had done. You don't have 800 kids without doing the publicity right! The program had the right mix of the ingredients discussed in the last chapter. And the purpose, theme, and goal were clear even to a casual observer. It didn't surprise me, then, that when I gave the opportunity to respons hugh numbers of kids did. Leaders and core kids were stepping forward to talk to their friends.

As a speaker, it sure is fun to speak in a situation like that. As I reflected on so many of the things that Stuart had done right, I recalled all the other times before when I had been told how many kids were expected, and when I got to the meeting, that number could be cut by three-fourths. As I reveled in the moment, I thought about how many times I had had to dig myself out of a hole when I got up to speak because the music was terrible, or the video didn't work, or the meeting was ill-conceived from the beginning. As I watched the counseling, I remembered meetings where total chaos reigned because the leaders weren't prepared for the response. Catching Stuart's eye, I smiled and winked. I gave him two thumbs up. I was in a youth communicator's paradise. I was having fun!

Let's finish figuring out how to structure your event so yours can have the same quality Stuart's had.

Music. Surrounding students every day, music reaches into their emotions and communicates to them in a way distinct from all other verbal expression. Since music permeates the student culture in modern America, it seems like an obvious move to capitalize on students' natural receptivity by weaving it into our presentation of Christ.

Music is a delicate tool. If performed excellently, it can contribute a special quality to the outreach event like nothing else can. But if executed poorly, it can cripple the entire meeting. *Quality* is the operative word. Quality has to do with *talent*. The people on your music team must be able to produce musically. Quality also has to do with *worship*. So much of what kids get today is entertainment, even from Christian musicians. Yet kids greatest need is to learn to encounter God in worship. The musicians who can help kids, believers and seekers, do that will win the day.

Using a mix of acceptable popular secular music, contemporary Christian music, and worship choruses will help create a comfortable and familiar atmosphere for secular students, but it will also stretch them to reach out to God in worship. You may think that non-Christian kids won't sing. Not. Their involvement in singing goesback to the quality. You may need to reach an understanding with your church on this issue, so think through your stance beforehand to avoid controversy and misunderstanding. I know significant controversy exists today over music in the church. If this issue looms large for you, please read Steve Miller's book *The Contemporary Christian Music Debate*, available from Tyndale House.

Select Your Options. Since youth groups vary in their range of talent, evaluate where you are and decide which of the following approaches you will use in your situation; then put your music team together.

• The Lead Musican. You need at least one person who can effectively lead kids in singing. He will be up front consistently and will carry a portion of the meeting. As well, he will coordinate the music each time you do an outreach event. He is the one to whom all of the other musicians are accountable. Therefore, this person must have talent and some leadership ability.

• Instruments. If you have the talent to do so, put together a group of students who play instruments—guitars, piano, synthesizer, drums.

• Band. Build the first two elements into a band by adding some more singers and then blending the sound of all of these together. Be careful here. Your lead musican is key in creating the sound you want. You do not want to sacrifice quality just to have a band up front. But if you have the people to pull it off, give it a shot. You might consider not only using kids, but also college students, and adult leaders. Another option is to recruit a band from another church or even another town to come and help you. You will need to work out an agreeable contract with them.

• Soloists. Weave these people into the music and the meeting when a solo will express your theme best.

• Tapes. If your group is small or not musically talented, you can rely on tapes and music videos. In this case have someone act as a disc jockey playing a selection of music videos and/or tapes.

• Guest Musicians. Inviting a guest will give variety and create an air of excitement. If the musician is particularly well-known, you can create publicity to take advantage of that. You will have to decide, in light of your goal, how much music you want the guest to do—from one number to a full concert. Make sure that your guest understands that this is not about performance, but about participation. Request that the students be brought into the music.

Music Preparation. To have quality music you must prepare. Consider these issues in your preparation.

• Equipment. Depending on what you already have, consider purchasing a good sound system with all auxiliary equipment. Buy a system that is larger than the one you presently need so you won't outgrow it too quickly. Consider its flexibility, adaptability, and transportability. Other basic equipment you will need in due time: music for the band, overhead projector, video projector, multimedia equipment.

• Budget. According to what you want to accomplish in music, set a budget figure. In your budget, build in the cost of all of the equipment above. Note: You do not need all of this to begin. You can purchase it gradually. Some of it your kids will have, and some you can borrow.

• Overhead copyright permission. For the sake of integrity, get permission from the music companies who have the copyright on the music. Simply write letters asking for permission. With that taken care of, then ask someone with a graphics program on their computer to type the overheads so they look really sharp. Type the words out in *large* letters so kids can read them on the overhead. Equipment is available to do all kinds of high-tech magic with things like rear projection and character generation. If you have the budget to do the high-tech stuff, contact Technical Industries for information. (See the address below.)

• Musicians. For the musicians to communicate effectively, they must prepare musically and spiritually. Musically, hold them accountable to practice a certain number of hours each week. Have them follow the charts in "The Outreach Event Planner" on pages 199–200 in order to coordinate their musical selections with the theme of the event. Spiritually, since these students are so visible to their peers, they need to be healthy, growing Christians. To help them keep an attitude that they are not performers, but servants, allow them to lead in music only if they are in a discipleship group. You may want to consider a discipleship group for the musical team. Another important step for continued spiritual health for the group is to have an extended period of time to pray before the event. Don't wait until the last minute to do this and then allow it to get squeezed out. Make prayer a priority.

The Event. Once prepared, what does the musical team do at the event? Use these suggestions to help the musical team function effectively at the event.

• Play musical transitions. Play the instruments between songs so the flow of the music is not interrupted. Avoid dead spots. Don't allow the musicians to talk between songs. Make these transitions as quickly as possible.

• Involve students. Since "hands on" participation is an important value, make sure the musicians get the kids involved. They have to model this participation for the kids. If they want them to clap their hands, stomp their feet, snap their fingers or whatever, then the musical leaders need to set the pace. Then think of creative ways to involve the kids. One music team has an old guitar with no strings. The leaders invite a series of students to come up and help play. Figure out fun and creative ways to get students "into it."

• Learn new songs. Nothing is more boring than to sing the same songs over and over every week. And nothing is more frustrating than singing a new song and then going on before it is learned. Somewhere in here is a balance. To teach a new song, prominently display the words on the screen. Announce that it is new. Take time to sing it through for them. Sing it through several times until they get the hang of it. Use it several weeks in a row until it is not new anymore

• Worship the Lord. That is the bottom line of what we are trying to do with the music. Worship does not have to be soft and quiet to honor the Lord. Help kids worship God with their own music, even the ones who don't know Him—yet!

Resources:

- Benson Music Group, 365 Great Circle Dr., Nashville, TN 37228. 615-742-6875.
- Carport Sound, 3705 Wyatt, Texarkana, TX 75503. 903-832-4080.
- CCM Communications, 107 Kenner Ave, Nashville, TN 37205. 615-386-3011. Publishes *Contemporary Christian Music Magazine.*
- Integrity Music, P.O. Box 16813, Mobile, AL 36616.
- Interl'inc, 5295 Crown Dr., Nashville, TN 37064. 615-790-9080.
- Maranatha! Music, P. O. Box 1396, Costa Mesa, CA 92626.
- Scripture in Song, P.O. Box 525, Lewiston, NY 14092.
- Songs and Creations, P.O. Box 7, San Anselmo, CA 94979-0007. 415-457-6610.
- Word, Inc, 5221 N. O'Connor Blvd. #1000, Irving, TX 75039. 214-556-1900.
- Young Life Songbook, P.O. Box 520, Colorado Springs, CO 80901.

Message. "It is a sin to bore kids with the Gospel," said Jim Rayburn, founder of Young Life. Certainly Jesus never bored people. When He spoke, He had such power and authority that His words changed people's lives. The apostles presented the message of Christ in such clear, natural, enthusiastic and bold expressions that their words pulsated with power and life. For them Jesus Christ was always the focal point. And our messages to kids through the Holy Spirit must have the same power and life that characterized the words of Jesus and the apostles.

To express the message of Christ powerfully to students, we must communicate through two channels—verbal and nonverbal.

Nonverbal Communication. I hear students say, "I don't remember what you talked about, but when you spoke that night it changed my life." They are saying that they "feel" the message of Christ more than they understand it intellectually. Adolescents are more "feelers" than "thinkers." Therefore, nonverbal communication of actions, attitudes, intensity, enthusiasm, and the quality of my life in Christ will come across more strongly than any particular words.

Positive nonverbal communication springs from five places in your life and ministry.

• Attitudes. Since attitude communicates more than anything else when we stand in front of kids, our attitudes are crucial. What attitudes do kids catch from you—love or harshness, kindness or cruel humor, patience or yelling at them, joy or anger, faith or cynicism? Our goal is defined by the Apostle Paul: "The attitude you should have is the one that Jesus Christ had" (Phil. 2:5). Make it your daily prayer that the Lord would conform your attitudes to His. Then when you communicate with kids the attitudes of Christ will come out.

• Reflection. When you know God, your kids will want to know Him. When you love God, your kids will want to love Him. When you hunger for Him, so will your kids. To deepen your passion for Him, build a special time with God into your schedule every day. Begin with 30 minutes a day for 30 days to make it a habit. As you reflect on Him, you will reflect Him when you get with kids. In fact, as this habit deepens and expands, you will find that almost all of your messages to students will come from notes, thoughts, and answered prayers from this time. As you experience God, you will desire to pass that experience on to your kids.

• Ministry. To speak to kids at the point of their need, we must live in their world. Spending time with them every week outside the context of the church will put you in touch with their needs. As you experience life on campus first hand, you will have a feel for what topics to speak on, what points will be relevant and what illustrations will inspire them. Then when you speak, they will listen. Why? Because you are interested in them personally, and you understand life on their level.

• Prayer. Prayer releases power when you speak. Pray for the students to whom you will speak. Praying will develop a deep compassion for them. Set aside at least one hour each week before you speak to connect the students you will speak to with the message you will deliver.

• Anointing. Ask God to pour out a special portion of His Spirit as you speak. He will only do that when your motives and goals are for His glory only. Ask the Lord to make your messages like the Apostle Paul's when he said, "My message and my preaching were not with wise and persuasive word, but with a demonstration of the Spirit's power, so that your faith might not rest on men's wisdom, but on God's power" (1 Cor. 2:4-5). Begin to pray for that anointing every day. When you speak in His anointing, God's Spirit will flow through you in power to students.

Verbal Communication. Lies bombard students from every angle: media, music, peers, even teachers. To overcome these lies with the Truth is our task. When we speak we want them to "know the truth, and the truth will set you free" (John 8:32).

Many youth leaders question their adequacy to stand before kids and proclaim the Truth. But one of your primary roles is to be a proclaimer of the Truth—to explain the Word of God to kids. Your gifts and talents may or may not lie in the area of proclaiming. YOU ARE STILL A TRUTH PROCLAIMER! Speaking is the verbal extension of living. Public speaking is a broader extension of private speaking. When you speak, Christ living in you will speak. For that reason, speaking is miraculous, supernatural. The Holy Spirit can communicate through you and call for a changed life.

Speaking is truth coming through your personality—your convictions, your walk with God, your mind, your spirit, your body. It takes hard work to learn to speak to kids effectively. I'm convinced, however, that if you can speak to kids effectively, you can speak to anybody!

To move toward powerful verbal communication, you will want to keep three simple principles in mind that will guide your speaking.

• Simplicity. "Keep the cookies on the lower shelf where everyone can reach them" needs to be our approach. The man on the street understands only two percent of the words in the dictionary, and the educated man understands only three percent. In speaking to students remember the familiar KISS approach: "Keep it simple, stupid."

• Authority. Your authority to speak to students comes from your walk with Christ, your understanding of the Scripture, your rapport with kids, and the release of the Holy Spirit in you. When you bring this to your speaking you *will* have credibility.

• Focus. One man said, "Nothing is so dangerous as to preach about God and perfection and not to point the way which leads to perfection." Make Jesus Christ the heart and soul of every message.

This combination of verbal love and nonverbal truth will make a powerful impact on students when you speak.

Preparing the Message. When I stand before a group of students to present the good news of Jesus Christ, I feel an awesome responsibility. When you speak to them, I know you feel it too. The Apostle Paul sensed that responsibility as well when he said, "We speak as men approved by God to be entrusted with the gospel. We are not trying to please men but God, who tests our hearts" (1 Thess. 1:4). The following practical, technical steps will help you prepare to fulfill this awesome responsibility.

• Plan ahead. In order to get the big picture on your messages, plan in advance. Put together a long-range plan. At the beginning of each year, sketch out your yearly speaking plan. Get by yourself and then with your outreach event team to pray through and fill out the "Message Plan." In working on your weekly plan, use the "Message Outline." You will find both of these in "The Outreach Event Planner" on pages 199 and 202.

Commit yourself to study. Do your homework. Just as teachers know if students do their homework, your students will know if you do yours. Spend no less than five hours preparing each message, using the standard of Colossians 3:23, "Whatever you do, work at it with all your heart, as working for the Lord, not for men."

• Choose the topic. Writing down the topics relevant to students can create a long list. In order to determine what topics you will speak on over the year, survey your group to discover its real and felt needs. Think through what you talk about when you have conversations and do counseling with your kids. Ask them to write down the 10 most important issues they face in their lives. Then, prayerfully, select your topics using the "Message Plan" on page 199.

• Focus on one passage. A topical approach can make rather superficial use of the Bible unless you focus on one passage. Digging into one passage exposes your kids to the richness and depth of the Bible. As you study the passage in your quiet time, use the Bible Response Sheet in "The Outreach Event Planner" on page 204. To study the passage in preparation for your message, use the "Message Research" on page 201.

Brainstorm ideas. Put down every idea that comes to your mind as you read through the passage. View the passage from the perspective of the characters in the story or the writer. Let the ideas flow as you read the passage again and again.

Ask questions. Read the passage again asking the questions who, what, where, when, why and how. Try to understand every word, action and thought.

Check the cross references. Following these through the Scripture will give you a feel for what God is saying about these verses through the entire Bible.

Check objections. Think about the questions your students will have about the topic and the passage, and answer those questions on paper.

Read the scholars. This is your last step, not your first one. You will be tempted to take the easy way out and get the scholars' viewpoint first. This is like eating food that someone else has chewed! Your best insights will come from what the Lord shows you, not what He has shown someone else. And by the time you get to this point, you will have more material than you can possibly use. Check the commentaries to make sure your ideas are not off base. My two favorite commentaries are The Tyndale New Testament Commentaries and *The Daily Study*

Bible by William Barclay, although a wide selection exists for you to choose from.

Knowing the passage thoroughly will give you confidence when you speak, and will establish credibility with the audience.

• Select one point. To clearly state your point, write down a goal statement. Use this little tool to help you:

"Every _____can/should_____."

For example, using the sample talk on parents in "The Outreach Event Planner" on page 205, the goal can be: "Every teenager can respond to his or her parents as Jesus did."

That one statement will determine what you include and exclude from your talk, and keep your talk on target as you prepare.

• Use powerful illustrations. Students will remember your illustrations long after they have forgotten the points of your talk. Illustrations will make your message come alive. You can select your illustrations in this descending priority order.

Firsthand experience. The best illustrations come from personal experience. For me, it was the time I got caught in the electronic door at the airport, or my basketball experience in college. What happens to you in everyday life will serve as your richest source of illustrations.

Secondhand experience. Stories about other people you know, stories they tell you, provide your second-best source of illustrations. For example, I can tell about how my friend Tommy grew up with an alcoholic father, or how a girl in the youth group of a friend of mine was healed after a severe accident.

Book experiences. To make these work you have to pick the inspiring ones that are down on the students' level. For example, I love to tell the story from Chuck Colson's *Loving God,* of Telemachus, a monk who as one individual stood against the Roman Empire and through his death stopped the carnage of the gladiators forever. Told in descriptive terms, it serves as a powerful illustration about standing alone for Christ.

• Write the message. To ensure clarity, and to facilitate the future use of this message, write it out first in outline form and then sentence by sentence, paragraph by paragraph. As you write, break it into three elements, using your goal statement to guide you.

Introduction. A good introduction gets you out of the blocks by arousing the interest of the students and getting the group involved from the start. Try one of these communication devices to effectively open your talk.

Ask a question. For example, "Do you think Jesus Christ ever had problems with His parents?"

Tell a personal experience. Share something funny or embarrassing that relates to your topic. For example, when I talk about peer pressure, I read the menu from "The Roadkill Grill" and then talk about how kids in the middle of the road are set up to be spiritual roadkill.

Involve kids in a demonstration. Bring kids up and get them to help you illustrate your point. For example, I love to bring up one guy who weighs 165 pounds and one who weighs about 85. The big one presses over his head the little one. Then I bring up someone over 200 pounds. The 165-pounder presses him (or tries too). My point: God is so great and mighty that you can't press Him, you can't control Him.

In the introduction make certain that you establish the point you want to focus on throughout the rest of the talk.

Body. Spend about three-fourths of your time developing the passage that illuminates your topic. These suggestions will help you make your message clear aand memorable.

Make one point clearly.

Outline your message concisely.

Explain the Scripture simply.

Use illustrations powerfully.

Prepare thoroughly.

Often it helps students to follow if you either give a handout or prepare an overhead with your outline on it. You will find an example of that in "The Outreach Event Planner" on page 206.

Conclusion. Restate your main point and then *apply* it. *Apply* is the operative word. The kids need to walk away knowing exactly what to do as a result of what they have heard. When your conclusion is clear, then your message is pinpointed for the kids. They can walk away saying exactly what the message was about. In an outreach event I have found it very positive to end with a question, repeated several times. For example, if the message is on sex and I've talked about how far is too far, then

I can pose the question: "How far is too far for you?" You can instruct your core kids to use the final question as a discussion starter with their friends to talk about Christ on the way home or during the week.

Use the Message Outline in "The Outreach Event Planner" to help you with these steps. See the Sample Message Outline in "The Outreach Event Planner" to get a feel for how to put the outline together so kids will remember your points.

• Learn the message. Once you have the entire manuscript written, work back through it.

As you consider how the students will hear it, trim out the irrelevant material or rephrase it to relate to the way they will understand it best.

Get the outline and illustrations firmly planted in your mind. Memorize your outline.

Pray through each point, asking the Holy Spirit to anoint it and to use it powerfully.

• Deliver the message correctly. A few basic reminders about public speaking will help you to communicate with the fewest distractions. Do these well and your speaking skills will improve dramatically.

Relax! Be yourself.

Establish eye contact. Look at individuals in the audience. Scan the room frequently, front to back, side to side.

Speak distinctly. Do a sound check beforehand to get the right amplification level. Make sure you can be heard clearly by those in the back of the room.

Communicate enthusiasm. A high energy level and a fast pace capture and retain the audience's attention.

Speak simply. Use simple language that everyone in the audience can understand.

Commend your listeners. People don't change in an environment of criticism, only in an environment of encouragement.

Love the audience. As you let the love of Christ flow out through you, they will sense it and respond.

Take your time. Pause after certain important points to let your point sink in. Use silence, pauses, and proper timing to bear down on important points.

Listen to the members of your audience. Watch their reactions to your words. Be flexible to adjust your talk to their responses.

Follow the leading of the Holy Spirit. As you speak, the Spirit will guide you to leave out a point, to include a new idea, to slow down or speed up.

- Evaluate the message. Critiquing your own message is not easy. Set aside a brief time the next day to reflect on the message. Be honest with yourself. Get a couple of people whose opinions you respect to advise you on how to improve. Tape the message and listen to it to discover how to make it better. Try to hone in on one thing you can improve on between now and the next time you speak. Use the Message Evaluation in "The Outreach Event Planner" on page 207 to help you.

When you have completed these steps, then you are ready to stand before students in a powerful, authoritative, convicting manner and proclaim the good news of Jesus Christ.

Resources:

- Dynamic Communicator's Workshop, 6080 West 82nd Dr., Arvada, CO 80003. 303-425-1319. Offers excellent training that improves speaking skills.

- *Hot Talks,* edited by Duffy Robbins, Youth Specialties, 1224 Greenfield Dr., El Cajon, CA 92021. 1-800-776-8008. This is a youth speaker's sourcebook with talks and ideas from some of the best youth speakers.

- *How to Speak to Youth,* Ken Davis, Group Publishing, P.O. Box 481, Loveland, CO 80539. 303-669-3836.

Invitation. Invitations to come to Jesus Christ in the New Testament are as numerous as the people invited. Sensitive to the needs of people, the inviter designed each invitation uniquely for that situation.

Looking at the invitations given in the New Testament, we see that they fall into three broad categories. People were invited to *come* (Matt. 11:28; 16:24; John 7:37). Others were invited to *go* (Matt. 19:21; John 8:11). Still others were encouraged to *believe* (Acts 2:37-38; 16:31).

We need to have the same sensitivity and uniqueness that the New Testament conveys when inviting students to come to Christ. No matter what approach we use, the invitation is for those without Christ to receive

Him. We can't make disciples, build the body, equip the saints, or grow the church if we do not first invite people to Christ. The invitation becomes the very important knob that allows people to walk through the door to Jesus Christ. With that in mind, then, we need to extend the invitation at every outreach meeting.

Four words help us define the invitation:

(1) Clarity. To ensure a long-lasting, fruit-bearing response, clarify what you are inviting your listeners to do. Usually I try to state that at the beginning of the message, somewhere in the middle, often at the end of each point, and at the end of the message. Write what you are inviting them to do in one sentence on your speaking notes.

(2) Reflection. In quietness give kids the opportunity to reflect on what they have just heard and to answer for themselves, "How does Jesus Christ relate to my life?" Then, rather than a shallow, emotion-filled response, they will make a deep, serious decision.

(3) Response. In some way students need to answer the question, "What do I need to do?" The invitation gives kids the opportunity to move out on that question.

(4) Application. The invitation should encourage students to take specific action as a result of the message. Usually that will fall into two categories: receiving Jesus, or making Jesus Lord of an area of their lives specifically addressed in the message.

With the invitation defined, we have the option of offering four different kinds of invitations, depending on the situation.

(1) Come forward. Used traditionally in crusades and rallies, this invitation has the advantage of calling kids to courageously step out in front of their peers and take a stand for Jesus Christ. Used properly it can evoke a deep, solid commitment from kids. The problem is that it has been misused and overused, and as a result lost some of its effectiveness. Rather than an everybody-who-can-spell-'God'-come-on-down invitation, you want to use this when you are giving a very narrow and specific appeal. Thinking out your exact approach ahead of time, explain to the kids exactly what you are asking them to do. You need to consider how to use it so kids will not be embarrassed, and so they will receive the proper counseling when they come.

(2) Fill out the card. At the end of the talk everybody fills out a card, including leadership, core kids, and visitors. They leave the card

in their seat. The follow-up team picks up the cards and sorts through them. Students who indicate they accepted Christ, or that they want to talk about their relationship to Christ, need someone from the follow-up team to make an appointment with them. The quicker the appointment, the more positive the response. The appointments can be scheduled during the outreach time explained in the chapter on preparation. This option is good only to the degree that you have trained people committed to the follow-up process. To have a stack of cards, which represent people's eternal destiny, sitting on someone's desk for several weeks doesn't cut it. Use this invitation only if you have a team doing immediate follow-up.

(3) Counseling room. At the close of the meeting, people who have made a decision to follow Christ or who want to talk about it, can come to a designated room, or corner of the big room. Trained counselors are in that room to talk to students. The disadvantage to this is that peer pressure can keep kids away. The advantage is that they are taking the initiative to seek help. You may consider using this one all of the time in conjunction with one of the other options. That way the kids know they can talk to someone any time they need to.

(4) Divide and conquer. When the speaker has asked the specific question at the end of his message, then the core kids who have been trained to handle this say immediately to a friend they have brought: "And how would you answer the question he asked?" Let them talk. When the friend finishes talking, have them say, "Can I tell you how I would answer the question?" and give their response. Then the Christian student asks, "Have you ever asked Jesus Christ to control your life or are you still thinking about it?" From that point they ask, "Could I share with you briefly how I received Jesus Christ?"

In my opinion this approach has the most effectiveness because it hands evangelism back to the students. They have a personal relationship with the friends they brought and they have prayed for their friends. For this to work you have to have a strong core of kids who have a genuine burden to reach their friends for Christ.

You can use any one of these approaches or a combination of them. As you consider your approach make certain that you have planned creatively so this will come off smoothly, maximizing what the Holy Spirit is doing in these kids' lives.

Resources:

- *The Facts of Life,* a booklet to explain the Gospel and lead kids to Christ. Order from Reach Out Ministries, 1-800-473-9456.

- *Getting Started,* a six-week follow-up tool to help new believers get established in their relationship with Jesus Christ. Order from Reach Out Ministries, 1-800-473-9456.

Follow-Up. *Don't let people slip through the cracks.* Because of a lack of planning in this area, often the wonderful things God did in the outreach event are lost or diminished. Continual care will greatly encourage the new believer's success in the Christian life. It takes time, energy, effort, and consistent love for a new believer to become enfolded into the body of Christ. Our objective here is not just to get kids to make decisions, but to help them become disciples. The Apostle Paul places focused energy at this point when he says,

> We proclaim Him, admonishing and teaching everyone with all wisdom, so that we may present everyone perfect in Christ. To this end I labor, struggling with all his energy, which so powerfully works in me. (Col. 1:28-29)

With this serious business in mind, how do we do it effectively? These practical suggestions will help you implement successful follow-up and counseling.

(1) First-time visitors. Follow-up begins with each visitor who attends the outreach event. The week after they visit they should receive:

- A letter thanking them for coming.

- A *Facts of Life* booklet with a challenge in the letter to read it.

- A visit by a person who has a relationship with him during the outreach time. This contact gives the first-time visitor an opportunity to hear the Gospel and respond. This personal attention will communicate a sense of concern and will build a bridge to the youth group.

(2) Second-time visitors. Once a student attends your outreach event the second time, have his friends call him and invite him to the youth group meeting at your church or to an evangelistic discussion held at school. (See *Taking Your Campus for Christ* for material to lead these discussion groups.)

(3) New Christians. When a student responds to Christ at an outreach event, then immediate follow-up must take place. The percentage of people who follow through with Christ is much higher if each person receives immediate attention. The student who led this person to Christ should meet with him two or three times the first week and then once a week after that. If, for some reason, that student cannot meet with the new Christian, then immediately assign him to someone else. The following steps will bolster the new convert.

- Review *The Facts of Life* booklet in detail, explaining each point and looking up each reference. This repetition will give him a better understanding of what happened to him when he received Christ.

- Give him the *Getting Started* booklet and work through the first session with him so he will feel comfortable doing it. Give him two days to finish that lesson, then get with him again for session two. Go all the way through the *Getting Started* booklet this way.

- Give the new Christian a Bible. Even if he has one already, this is a nice gift that helps nail down the decision for him. Challenge him to begin reading the Gospel of Mark.

- Involve him in the ministry the kids have at school and in the activities at the church.

Resources:

- *The Facts of Life,* a booklet to explain the Gospel and lead kids to Christ. Order from Reach Out Ministries, 1-800-473-9456.

- *Getting Started,* a six-week follow-up tool to help new believers get established in their relationship with Jesus Christ. Order from Reach Out Ministries, 1-800-473-9456.

Counseling. Kids live in incredible pain. They need to work through not only their new decision for Christ, but also the problems and struggles they are having that could keep them from going on with Christ. Having a counseling resource is essential for youth ministry today. Use the counseling room option discussed above to give kids a doorway to get help. Then train counselors in how to deal with the issues. You will want to build a counseling team of professional counselors, trained lay volunteers, and peer counselors. (See the resources below.)

In order for what we have discussed in follow-up and counseling to work, we have to train people. You knew it wouldn't happen magically! Scheduling time to do this and then having kids take the time to follow-up will present one of your biggest hurdles. But this has great value in that it teaches students how to take responsibility for *their* ministry. To nail down the scheduling, set up these four options.

(1) Have a counselor training seminar. Do this Saturday morning or another time if it suits your schedule better. In this clinic, teach them how to follow up. Hopefully you will have a large group who will want to do this. Cover the following issues and have them practice on each other.

- Decisions. Go over the invitations above and discuss the types of decisions that students make and how to handle each one. Help them see the importance of going over the decisions to receive Christ even if those students go to church. No person should ever assume by appearances only that a student is a Christian. Show counselors how to work through this issue by asking the person they are witnessing to "What do you think it means to be a Christian?" and "How has following Christ worked out in a practical way in your life?"

- Testimony. Teach counselors how to write down and express their personal testimony.

- Gospel. Show them how to go through *The Facts of Life* booklet.

- Bible. Show them how to give away the Bible as a gift, then how to help a new Christian know where to start and how to read it.

- Follow-up. Show them how to work through the *Getting Started* booklet. Have them work through all of the lessons. Help them work out when they will do this in their schedules. Provide the outreach time each week as a regular opportunity to get this done.

- Difficult problems. If a problem is more complex than leading a person to Christ, show counselors how to refer it to you, your adult leaders, the peer counseling team or a professional counselor.

(2) Have a "Giving Away Your Faith" discipleship group. In it teach your kids in-depth how to lovingly and boldly share Christ with their

friends. Take them through *Giving Away Your Faith* by Barry St. Clair over a 10-week period. They will learn every aspect of how to communicate Christ in this experience.

(3) Set up a 10-session training course to train your core kids to be peer counselors. Use *Peer Counseling* and *Advanced Peer Counseling* to show them how to help their friends who are having problems.

(4) Have a weekly outreach time. Use the first 10 minutes of this time each week to teach or review something with the kids that has to do with sharing their faith, follow-up, or counseling. Make it "hands on" and let them practice it.

When a student leads one of his fellow students to Christ, follows him up, or takes responsibility to help with a problem, you will see a high degree of motivation and a dramatic increase in the growth of his own life. No more of this "Our kids are apathetic." When they see God use them they will be fired up and their faith will deepen. Use this opportunity to its fullest potential.

Resources:

- *The Facts of Life,* Reach Out Ministries, 1-800-473-9456.

- *Getting Started,* Reach Out Ministries, 1-800-473-9456.

- *Taking Your Campus for Christ,* Reach Out Ministries, 1-800-473-9456.

- *Giving Away Your Faith,* Reach Out Ministries, 1-800-473-9456.

- *Peer Counseling* and *Advanced Peer Counseling,* Joan Sturkie and Siang-Yang Tan, Youth Specialties, 1224 Greenfield Dr., El Cajon, CA 92021. 1-800-776-8008.

- *Counseling Teenagers,* G. Keith Olsen, Group Books, P.O. Box 481, Loveland, CO 80539. 303-669-3836.

- RAPHA, P.O. Box 580355, Houston, TX 77258. 1-800-227-2657 or 1-800-45-RAPHA. RAPHA provides excellent Christ-centered professional counseling for teenagers.

- New Life Treatment Centers, 570 Glennere Ave., #107, Laguna Beach, CA 92651. 1-800-227-LIFE. New Life Treatment Centers also provide biblically-based professional counseling for young people.

When you have invested the time and effort to implement all of the ministries designed in these two chapters you will have one incredible outreach ministry to your community.

ACTION POINTS

1. Work through "The Outreach Event Planner" material for this chapter.

2. Schedule an outreach event.

Nine

Hit the Road, Jack:
Mobilizing Students for Action

Dashing in the door, he grabbed a quick bite to eat before he headed out the door. He had just come in from a day that started at 7:00 A.M. with a 35-minute drive to school, and ended after basketball practice and another 35-minute maneuver through the traffic. So after such a long day, where was he going? "Gotta get to NiteLife. We've got a skit tonight and I need to make sure everything is ready." My son Scott went through that routine every week, because he knew that he was part of something fun, something with his friends, and something that was bringing students to Christ every week. When he got home, he would give a detailed report about what happened to "Ned (the Nerd) Newschool" in his skit and people who had accepted Christ.

What makes a kid who already has more to do than he should have, make that sacrifice to get to that crazy outreach event? Simple. He was motivated by a youth leader with a vision to reach kids for Christ, and who mobilized his kids to do the same. The leader wasn't foolish enough to think he could do it all himself. No, he let the kids own the meeting. From bringing their friends to running the program, they did it all except for the speaking (and sometimes they would even do that).

All we have worked on in this book will go down in flames unless the kids own it. But when they do, they will get off of their duffs of apathy and onto the front line of ministry.

131

And what about you? When you let other people own it, where does that leave you?

One night I was scheduled to speak at a very large church with a very large outreach event. The youth pastor picked me up at the airport, took me to my motel, casually ate dinner with me, then took me to the church. The meeting started in forty-five minutes. He gave me a tour of their youth facilities, introduced me to several people. When the meeting started he sat beside me filling me in on what was happening and why they did each of the segments of the program. The entire evening all he did was introduce me. He did not have one, single responsibility except to introduce the speaker! WOW! How did he do that? He shared ownership!

For most of us this is very difficult. We have not learned how to delegate well. Usually that is because we don't think someone else will do as good a job as we would. It seems easier to take the approach: "I'll just do it myself." That may work in the short run. But in the long run not only will you burn out, but also you miss a prime opportunity to develop future leadership.

Why do so many adult leaders drop out of youth ministry? Apathetic kids. Why do so many kids drop out? Adult-dominated ministry. How many juniors and seniors are actively involved in your meetings? Where are they? Why aren't they there? Because we are still trying to spoon-feed them like we did when they were in the first grade. They need the opportunity to flex their spiritual muscles, to take on a challenge, to try out their leadership wings. That's why it is critical for them to own the outreach event.

So, hit the road, Jack! As you hit the road to take less ownership, challenge kids to hit the road to take more responsibility. The vehicle you are going to hit the road in we'll call the HIT Team.[1] The HIT Teams handle the various areas of responsibility for the outreach event. By continually being exposed to the responsibilities of planning and executing their tasks, they develop in spiritual leadership.

THE TEAM CONCEPT

Note that this is a team concept. A group of students, not just one person, is responsible for an area of ministry. An adult from your Leadership

Team will need to serve as leader/advisor for each team. The HIT Teams are formed, then, according to talents, gifts, and interests.

The number and size of the teams will depend on your youth group. Your mission is to involve every willing student on a HIT Team. When you do that you will experience some very positive benefits.

- Your load is lightened in administration so you have more time for building relationships and preparing messages.

- Students are more quickly reached by their peers than by adults.

- The decline in involvement in the later years of high school comes to a screeching halt.

- Students build confidence as they are stretched to take risks, and as they see lives changed as God works through them.

The Covenant. To serve on a HIT Team requires a commitment to a consistent ministry. One of the major character issues that kids will grow in is faithfulness—to take on a task and follow through with it. For that reason you will want to request that the volunteers sign the HIT Team Covenant. (See "The Outreach Event Planner" page 210.)

The Organizational Big Picture. The organizational chart for the outreach event is on the following page.

Over each student leader is an adult advisor. Under each student leader is a team of students.

The Planning Meetings. *The Leadership Meetings.* The HIT Team leaders get together in one meeting with two agendas.

- Plan ahead for the HIT Teams. This part of the meeting consists of putting together the "Getting Your Ducks in a Row" sheet. This needs to be done well in advance and on a timely basis so that each HIT Team will have the information they need to plan their part of the program.

- Set the final plan for the outreach event. A better portion of the time will be spent putting together the final program so that all of the right elements are present, and all of the parts fit together cohesively. They will need to work on transitions in the program as well. The "Program Cue Sheet," the "Rehearsal Schedule" and the "Technical Schedule" all are completed. (See "The Outreach Event Planner" page 211-220.) After this meeting, the program

The Outreach Event Organizational Chart

(Each student leader has an adult advisor)

Enlarge this page and complete

Event Leader
(The Youth Leader)
[   ]

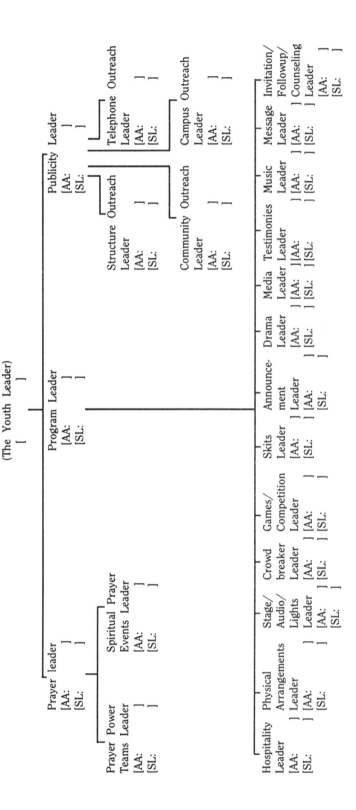

should be finely tuned. Any final assignments can be made that need to be carried out before the event.

The Team Meetings. Each team will meet weekly if you have a weekly outreach event, or at the appropriate time to plan for the outreach event.

- The HIT Team leaders will provide each team with the "Get Your Ducks in A Row" sheet already filled out for them down through #4.

- From that each team fills out #5-#6 as they brainstorm ideas and resources.

- They need to come out of that meeting with their "Individual HIT Team's Plan" sheet filled out. If the "Skit Team" has specific skits they want to bring to the table, then they need to have those skits in hand with a copy for everyone.

- Their part of the "Meeting Structure" sheet needs to be completed with the three specific contributions their team might make to the event. Obviously many of those plans will be amended as the planning gets more focused.

Here is a list of specific team responsibilities:

(1) Prayer Power Teams Team. Even though its name is a little awkward, this easily could be the most important team of all. It is responsible for

- beginning Prayer Power Teams on every campus with every person who wants to be in one.

- communicating with the Prayer Power Teams so they do not lose their motivation.

- furnishing the Prayer Power Teams with the specific prayer requests for the outreach event.

Review Chapter 4 for details.

(2) Special Prayer Events Team. This team's focused responsibility is to call the church and the young people to pray *for this specific event.* They carry out the special prayer plans discussed in chapter 4. This team is responsible for

- determining which prayer approach they will use for the event.

- laying out a specific plan for accomplishing that prayer strategy.

- coordinating the prayer plan with the church, youth ministry, and outreach schedule.

- carrying out the prayer plan.

(3) Structured Outreach Team. You and/or an adult leader need to have strong input. However, let the kids do most of the planning and organizing. This group will be responsible for maintaining your visible, ongoing evangelism structure. Its responsibilities include

- working with the youth leader to organize the outreach time to meet the needs of your unique situation.

- linking the partners each week.

- making assignments each week that allow the teams to see the people they have relationships with.

- designing a very accurate record-keeping system and keeping it up to date every week. Your church probably has a computer system that is adequate for this task. Plug into that.

(4) Telephone Team. The students who sign up for this need to have no fear of talking to strangers. They might need some training in telephone manners. This team is responsible for

- obtaining the phone directories of the various schools.

- training the team in how to use the survey.

- setting up a plan to distribute the numbers and make the calls. (The easiest approach is to photocopy the sheets from the directory and pass them out to the team.)

- keeping accurate records. Have each calling team be responsible for recording the results of their calls on the central record-keeping system.

(5) Campus Publicity Team. As this team is carrying out their responsibilities, it would help each person to read *Taking Your Campus for Christ.* Members' responsibilities include

- working with the youth leader on the "School Survey" in *Penetrating the Campus.*

- using the "School Survey" and the information in Chapter 6 to decide who your audience is and how you will target these people.

- communicating with the youth group about how they can get the word out person to person.

- communicating with the principal/administration to get permission to put up publicity and hand out fliers.

- designing, printing, and distributing the publicity pieces needed.

(6) Community Publicity Team. You will need some students on this team who are mature enough to relate to the adult community. They are responsible for

- coordinating their plans with the Campus Publicity Team so efforts won't be duplicated.

- writing a press release for the event. (See page 195.)

- going to the local newspaper and inviting them to do a story on the outreach event.

- calling radio and TV stations to request public service announcements for the event and exploring the possibilities of appearing on a local talk show or doing an interview.

- working with local businessmen to get them to sponsor some of your publicity efforts.

(7) Hospitality Team. Outgoing, friendly students who take initiative to welcome others should staff this team. Their responsibilities are

- deciding together how they will make people feel welcome. They will need to keep in mind important mixing skills such as remembering names, introducing people to each other, expressing a genuine interest in other people.

- spreading out in the parking lot, in the halls and around the room.

- making sure everyone is spoken to and included.

- spreading out during the meeting and entering into every activity with enthusiasm.

- speaking to as many people as possible when it is over, thanking them for coming and inviting them back again.

- providing refreshments when needed and appropriate.

- calling all of the first time visitors during the week.

(8) Physical Arrangements Team. People who sign up for this team need to take pride in the way things look. They will need to

- arrange the facility the way the youth leader wants it set.

- decorate the room so that it is warm and inviting.

- make sure all equipment is present: furniture, props, pencils, paper, invitation cards, book table, sign up table, handouts, overhead projector, transparencies, pens.

- complete all of this 30 minutes prior to the time to begin.

(9) Stage Team. This should consist of the people who are responsible for the lights, audio and video. They will be responsible for

- knowing the technical schedule thoroughly in order to have all sound and lights coordinated with the schedule.

- doing a sound/light/video check 30 minutes before the event begins.

- wiring the speaker with his microphone.

- preparing all overheads/graphics so they are sharp and large enough to be seen.

- taking down all lights/sound/video after the meeting and storing them properly.

(10) Crowdbreaker Team. Kids who know how to create high energy excitement need to sign up for this team. They need to

- research all of the crowdbreaker resources and gather them into a small library to have available every week. (They should work with the youth leader to secure the money for these books.)

- decide which crowdbreakers fit the theme and goal for the event.

- gather all of the equipment needed to make the crowdbreaker work.

- prepare, practice and carry out the crowdbreaker with excellence.

(11) Games/Competition Team. A variety of kids need to compose this team, not just the ones who are highly competitive. They are responsible for:

- researching all of the games/competition resources and gathering them into a small library to have available every week. (They need to ask the youth leader for help in purchasing these items.)

- deciding which games/competition fit the theme and goal of the event.

- determining the proper setting for the games (gym, large room, etc.).

- gathering all of the equipment needed for the games/competition.

- preparing, practicing and carrying out the games/competition with excellence.

(12) Skits Team. The kind of kids needed on this team are the ones who are not afraid to ham it up in front of people. They need to

- research all of the skits resources and gather them into a small library to have available every week. (Work with the youth leader on where to get the money for this.)

- decide which skits fit the theme and goal of the event.

- gather all of the equipment needed for the skits.

- prepare, practice, and carry out the skits with excellence.

(13) Announcements Team. You can combine this team with the skits team if needed. The kids on this team need to be creative, up-front people. Their responsibilities are

- brainstorming all of the different ways announcements can be done, then gathering any resources needed.

- getting the announcements from the appropriate person in writing, in order to know for sure the information they want to communicate.

- preparing the announcements creatively with skits, interviews, etc.

- practicing and carrying out the announcements with excellence.

(14) Drama Team. The students on this team either have some drama experience or have a real desire to get started in it. To do this well you will need a director who has dramatic skills. This person will determine the level of excellence with which this will be done. The Drama Team is responsible for

- researching and gathering all needed dramatic resources and making them available every week. (Work with the youth leader on how to pay for this.)

- clearing any necessary permission forms and fees with publishers.

- deciding realistically how many dramas you can do in a month.

- meeting with the youth leader to determine the theme and goal of the event.

- gathering all of the props needed for the drama.
- coordinating with the Light/Sound/Video Team their responsibilities for the drama.
- preparing, practicing, and carrying out the drama with excellence. Realize that this will take more time than needed by some other teams. Setting up times to rehearse.

(15) Media Team. The people on this team will need expertise in video and photography. They will need to

- gather all of the equipment needed to function properly. This can get expensive, so be creative. Use equipment that the church or a person is willing to lend. Gradually add to existing equipment so that the group doesn't need to depend on other people's equipment.
- determine what video/ photography footage and music resources are needed for the entire year so the use of it can be maximized.
- decide what video/photography you will need to fit the theme and goal of the event.
- videotape and photograph ball games, school events, interviews, retreats, camps, and any other events in which kids are involved.
- finish any presentation a day before the event so the leaders can review it and see how it fits the program.
- prepare and carry out the presentation with excellence.

(16) Testimonies Team. The people on this team are not the ones who give all of the testimonies. Rather they select the people who will give them and work on their testimonies with them. Their responsibilities include

- preparing their own personal testimonies according to the guidelines in *Giving Away Your Faith,* and presenting them in public.
- keeping an eye out for people in whose lives God is visibly working. They should ask these people to relate what God is doing in their lives. They should also keep a list of people who would make good candidates for delivering a testimony.
- determining what kind of testimonies fit into the theme and goal of the event. Use variety and creativity.
- selecting the people who will give the testimonies.

- rehearsing with the people who will give testimonies. Team members need to feel free to critique what is said and suggest improvements.

(17) Music Team. Obviously people with musical talent will make up this team. If you have only a few people with talent, go with those young men and women. If you have lots of talented people, then either make up two bands or shift people in and out. Music team members are responsible for

- researching all music resources and gathering them into a small library that can be available every week. Team members will have to be selective, choosing music that fits the kind of program you will do.

- meeting with the youth leader to get very specific directions on the kind of music he/she wants. Team member should search for cassettes or CDs that feature the sound they are looking for.

- creating a practice schedule for the team. Make certain that everyone is committed to being at the practices. The music team will have a more extensive commitment than most other teams. Everyone needs to make sure they can and will come to the practices.

- meeting with the youth leader to determine the specific theme and goal for the event.

- meeting with the Stage/Audio/Lights Team to communicate your needs.

- setting up all equipment two or three hours before the event.

- doing a sound check one hour before the event.

- practicing, preparing, and carrying out the music with excellence.

- coordinating the talents of any guest musicians with the closely-defined theme and goal of the event. Make them aware of the kind of music needed, the time they have, and the audience they will sing to. The team should help with their equipment, sound system, lights, and other needs they have.

(18) Message Team. The people on this team consist of the speakers. That will include the youth leader but also some others who have gifts in this area. Encourage people to join this team who aspire to communicate Christ and then give them an opportunity to do so. Message Team members are responsible for

- deciding how their messages fit into the overall theme and goal of the event.

- preparing and delivering the message at the outreach event. This may not always be in the form of a talk. Members should explore creative alternatives such as films, videos, interviews, panel discussions, or a variety of other formats.

- setting aside the time needed to prepare and practice.

- following the speaking suggestions on pages 122–123.

- critiquing the talk after it is over so everyone on the team learns how to do it better.

- assisting any guest speaker to know what is expected in topic, time, and meeting any other expectations.

(19) Invitation/Follow-up/Counseling Team. This team is not responsible for doing all of the counseling. Their main purpose is to train and prepare others who will either discuss the invitation with their friends, follow up with the people who respond, or do peer counseling in the counseling room. This team needs to

- prepare all resources needed for the invitation—cards, pencils, *Facts of Life* booklets, *Getting Started* booklets, New Testaments.

- meet with the speaker to decide how the invitation will be handled. Decide this on the basis of the theme and goal.

- train all of the counselors in three levels of training:

   (a) How to follow up at an event. This can be accomplished in a three-hour seminar.

   (b) How to share one's faith successfully. This can be accomplished by going through the 10-week *Giving Away Your Faith* discipleship group.

   (c) How to counsel one's peers. This can be accomplished in a 10-week peer-counseling course.

- secure access to professional counselors when needed. Check with your pastor and community resources for *Christ-centered* counselors. Make a list of names and phone numbers.

- show the counselors what to do and how to respond at the invitation. Meet with them for a few minutes after a youth group meeting to go over this. Give them all of the material at that time. If no public invitation is going to be given, remind them to discuss the question with the friends they brought.

When you have this many kids in direct front line ministry either weekly or on a regular basis, then you are definitely making a high impact!

ACTION POINTS

1. Create sign-up, ideas, and responsibility sheets for each of the nineteen teams. See "The Outreach Event Planner" for examples of these forms. If you do not have enough students to fill up these teams, then figure out which teams you need the most and design sheets for those teams. You can combine several of the teams or leave out some in order to fit your situation.

2. Have students sign up to be on the teams. Take time to prepare and publicize sign-up times. Set aside one meeting as the sign-up week, and then catch the kids who weren't there or weren't ready at the earlier meeting during the next meeting.

1. HIT stands for High Impact Team. This idea is taken from First Baptist Church North in Atlanta, Ga., where Andy Stanley is my pastor.

Ten

Play Together: Cooperating for Impact

Paul Fleischmann

Casey Stengel, manager of the world-champion New York Yankees, once said, "It's easy to get good players; getting them to play together—that's the hard part." There are many wonderful ministries and talented workers in each of our cities, but until we can get them working together, the fulfillment of the Great Commission in our communities will be stymied. As stated in the previous chapter, Jesus' prayer to His Father clearly indicates that it is the oneness of believers that will persuade people of the authenticity of our faith (John 17:20-26). Starting your own local network not only makes a statement to that effect, but also helps get people "playing together" as a team in a way that makes a far greater impact on a community than we could ever make alone.

ESTABLISH YOUR PURPOSE

There are approximately 200 local chapters of the National Network of Youth Ministries across the United States. The overall purpose of each chapter is to cooperate in such a way that *"every teenager can be exposed to the gospel, discipled toward a biblical lifestyle, established in a local church and equipped to help reach the world."* One of the specific goals is to see a ministry established to each junior and senior high school. Each local Network chooses how to best implement these purposes based on the needs and resources in their community.

It is important to have a stated objective if you hope to function effectively as a team. For example, the military objective of Operation

Desert Storm was to "Free Kuwait." This gave much-needed direction and unity to the vast variety of troops from many different countries who had to familiarize themselves with different military styles and strategies. Having a clear purpose (repeated publicly many times) made the difference between functioning as a powerful "allied force" or merely as a number of random armies.

Likewise, in youth ministry, we come from many different denominational backgrounds and a variety of contrasting ministry styles. If we merely operate independently, we may see some results, but nothing like what we could see if we agreed upon our objective and became an "allied force." Some of our local Networks are using the phrase, "Every Kid, Every Campus, Every Community" to remind them of their purpose. Like the phrase "Free Kuwait," it gives us a sense of focus and helps us screen everything we do through the filter of our purpose.

I have seen the results of networks with no clear objective to unite them. Right after I moved to San Diego, I tried to find a youth ministry network. To my surprise, despite the presence of many large, effective youth ministries, there was no regular gathering of youth workers. When I asked why, several said that they didn't have the time, and that frankly, they did not really see the need. I didn't push it, but kept asking around until I found several of us who did feel a need to meet together. We started gathering monthly at a "brown-bag" lunch meeting to share and pray together.

Our numbers stayed small for almost two years. At one meeting a youth pastor said that he had a need to provide training for some of his leadership kids and wondered if anyone else had that need. Most of us agreed and so we planned a weekend training where each of us took part of the responsibility. Later, one of the Youth for Christ staff suggested we get involved with one of their evangelistic events. We all agreed because we each wanted our students exposed to more quality opportunities for evangelism and saw how this would help everyone. In our own way we had finally stumbled upon a purpose. The San Diego Network grew quickly from that point, and has since co-sponsored many outreach events.

Many networks start this way—youth workers getting together just because they sense they should, but with no real sense of purpose. If the relationships aren't very strong and the purposes don't solidify soon, most networks will fizzle or be reduced to a type of clique. Let me suggest several steps to help you form a more stable network:

- Make a list of key youth workers you think would share a similar burden for young people.

- Meet with them one-on-one or for a meal in a comfortable setting.

- Discuss what needs they think youth leaders and young people have in your area. Prioritize the needs.

- Consider how cooperation in some areas might help you better meet those needs.

- Write some objectives you can agree upon. Start with an overall purpose (like the Network purpose above), and then develop sub-goals which will help you achieve that purpose. Do your best to combine reality and faith. You won't likely accomplish your purpose overnight, so start with reachable goals that will help you build momentum.

ORGANIZE LEADERSHIP

Once your purpose is clear, you can begin organizing to accomplish it. There is often a question of who should take the first steps. Most likely you should! Someone needs to get the ball rolling. It doesn't mean you have to be the permanent leader, but if you will take some key "first steps" you can help overcome the "initial inertia" which dooms many good ideas. Satan can't stop God from speaking to your heart, but he can persuade you to put it off until tomorrow, or pass it off as someone else's job. Reaching our communities is a vital part of Christ's Great Commission to us. We must not lose any more ground to the enemy, but rather be "redeeming the time, because the days are evil" (Eph 5:16). Here are some "key first steps:"

Determine Your Geographic Boundaries.

Normally, a network works best if its members are within a "comfortable traveling distance." You'll need to decide what that is. If there is no active network nearby, you may want to shoot for a larger scope to begin with, and then break it down as soon as more leadership surfaces. In southern California we started with just one Network and then gradually recruited a Network Coordinator for each of 21 communities. Today there are 10 Network areas in Orange County alone. This is a similar approach which has been used successfully in many metropolitan areas. But, wherever you live, the old military principle of "divide and conquer" is still very effective. Start where you are and continue to break down the area into bite-size pieces.

Develop Your Leadership Team.

Many local Networks have a life expectancy of two to three years when only one person serves as "the leader." He or she may be effective and may handle the extra effort and demands well, but it is important to consider the realities if this person "burns out," relocates or transitions into another role in ministry. Often the local Network is left hanging. That is why it is best to build your network around a leadership team or steering committee so that long-term vision and continuity of momentum can be sustained.

This team usually functions best when the specific roles are based on *task* not *position*. The most universal role in the Network is that of "Coordinator." As the name implies, he is not so much a "president" as he is one who helps coordinate the process of networking in the community. He is one who keeps us to the objectives and assists others in fulfilling their roles. Other roles on the team could be Assistant Co-ordinator (who may be preparing to assume the Coordinator role at the end of his term), Prayer Coordinator (*See You at the Pole*, etc.), Campus Coordinator (student-led clubs, "every campus" objective, etc.), Secretary/Treasurer (minutes, mailing list, etc.), Welcome Coordinator (contacts new youth workers, etc.), Project Coordinator (leads Network-sponsored outreach events, etc.)

Sow Broadly.

Once you have established a clear purpose and have your basic leadership in place, try to incorporate as many youth workers as possible. We are not just trying to go for large numbers for numbers sake. But since Jesus' Great Commission (Matt 28:18-20) and His prayer for our oneness (John 17:20-23) is so important to Him, it makes sense that we should try to gather all the resources available for the task. Part of our role in reaching our community is to "cast vision." We might think that some youth workers might not be interested, but cast the vision and find out. I've seen some youth workers come to Network meetings in a critical frame of mind, or not very interested in evangelism or prayer events—and then, over time, they warmed up so much you would think they had been transformed! I believe that involvement in a Network helps to shape people's ministry philosophy as they are exposed to what works, as they see the heart of God in others, and as they come to grips with the need to reach their community.

Have your Network leaders brainstorm to make a list of all the known youth leaders in the area. If they are believers who work with kids, and are not cult members, include them! Of course, churches and Christian youth organizations are the first ones that come to mind. But there are many other Christians working in youth-related jobs: school teachers, coaches and administrators, youth professors at seminaries and colleges, agents for Christian artists, counselors, workers at drug rehabilitation centers, juvenile facilities, YMCA/YWCA, urban ministry, pregnancy centers, youth hot lines, camps and conference centers, athletic programs, missions agencies, youth publications and media, and many more. When you start looking at the community as the Holy Spirit does, you will see a wealth of resources which, when He "networks" it, will be—like the loaves and fishes—more than enough to fulfill the Great Commission in our cities!

After you have drawn up your list, invite everyone to a Network meeting where you "cast the vision"—tell them what's on your heart, what's been accomplished so far, and what things could be done together in the future. Take ample time for input from them. Everyone should have the sense of being in on the "ground floor," that their suggestions are being heard, and that their own vision can be incorporated. Get consensus as to the next steps and then give them opportunity to sign up for some active involvement. Have a meaningful time in prayer.

These meetings can really be tremendous. I'll never forget a youth worker meeting we set up in the New York City area before they had an active Network. I asked a well-known youth leader to gather a group of youth workers for lunch who might be interested in networking. Twenty-five sharp youth workers shared noisily over lunch. Just before I was going to "cast the vision," I asked everyone to introduce themselves. That was all the further we got! Because most of the people were new to each other, the introductions served to open their eyes to much-needed resources right under their noses. And, boy, did they get excited! We hadn't been half way around the table when one youth pastor said, "This is just too good! We need to meet every month—and we can do it at my church three weeks from Saturday." Someone else offered their church, and then someone from Manhattan challenged us to meet there. The only problem we had was choosing where to meet. When it came my turn to talk, there was nothing more to be said. The vision had already been "cast"—and the results of the New York Network have continued ever since.

Develop a Strategy.

Devising a plan to reach every young person in your community may sound pretty overwhelming. But in a way, it's like setting up that first Network in southern California. You just start where you are. You don't have to accomplish it all today—rather, ask God what He would want you to do this year. As we are obedient to the promptings of his "still small voice" (1 Kings 19:12), He can take our "little" and make it "much." Think of the original planners of *See You at the Pole!* I don't think they envisioned it blowing into a firestorm of spiritual interest all across the world. But God's promise in Jeremiah 33:3 is that, when we call upon Him, He will "show us great and mighty things which you do not know." God seems to love to "break the mold!" Just be sure you seek Him for His plan—then venture out with anticipation.

As you examine the needs related to your overall purpose of reaching your community's youth, God will give you peace about which ideas will make up an effective strategy. Since the needs of your city are unique, your strategy will be unique, too. Here are some methods that have worked well in Networks across the country, especially in the area of cooperative evangelism.

Campus Outreach.

Prayer. See You at the Pole, already mentioned, is a great way to unite all the Christians at the beginning of the school year to pray for their friends, teachers, city and nation. *Prayer Triplets* keep that emphasis throughout the year as 3 friends meet 3 times a week, each praying for 3 non-Christian friends. *PG-13* is a program used in Colorado Springs with junior highers who are willing to meet on campus in a Prayer Group for 13 weeks. *Prayer Breakfasts* are used in New Jersey for Christian students to meet each week in order to pray for each other, their non-Christian friends, and some ministry of evangelism.

Evangelism Campaigns. Locker to Locker is a special week each year in Wichita, Kansas where students commit to pray over the lockers of 10 of their friends and then invite them to an evangelistic rally at the end of the week–thousands have received Christ each year! *The Book of Hope* is a teenage edition of the Gospels published in Cincinnati where 15,000 were distributed legally in schools by Christian students giving them personally to their friends.

Christian Campus Clubs. Approximately 10,000 student-led clubs are meeting on campuses each week as a result of the Equal Access Amendment. In Miami, 24 of the 26 schools have clubs which cut across church boundaries. The local Network provides *monthly training* for the student leaders and publishes a quarterly *newspaper.* In San Diego, the Network sponsored a *student leadership conference* to train club leaders and provide materials. In Birmingham, *First Priority* is a specific effort to network the students from the individual churches into one positive group on campus.

Assemblies. Though single churches may not be able to sponsor school assemblies, Networks have had good success in scheduling a variety of assembly programs since the Network usually represents a number of different denominations. In conjunction with *Locker to Locker,* the cooperating ministries in Wichita hosted assemblies in 73 schools. Cincinnati does a blitz of area schools almost every year. Usually programs must be very generic, featuring a star athlete, musician, comedian or perhaps covering a need like drug abuse. However, due to recent gang violence in Chicago, one area youth worker was allowed to give the Gospel and a come-forward invitation, to which 400 students and teachers responded.

Community-Wide Outreach.

Prayer. Prayer is also a big part of evangelism on a community-wide basis. *Yearbook pictures* were used to make up prayer cards for adults to use to pray daily for all the students in Rochester, Minnesota. A *Jericho Walk* starts out the monthly Network meeting in Los Angeles as youth workers make a "prayer lap" around a different campus each month. *Moms in Touch* has prayer groups of mothers praying for their children at thousands of schools, including junior and senior highs.

Evangelistic Crusades. Youth Night at various crusades are organized by networks. In Cincinnati, students started praying for specific friends three months in advance, received evangelism training, and followed up new converts at an all-night party. On Long Island, New York, where youth pastors are scarce, over 150 lay youth leaders cooperated in the Billy Graham Crusade. After the Portland, Oregon, Graham Crusade, over 200 youth workers continued to cooperate through six separate Networks. In Wichita, *Locker to Locker* concluded the week with a mass rally for 15,000. Five hundred parents circled the football stadium with a ring of prayer while 1,300 students made first-time decisions for Christ.

Outreach Events. *Operation: PowerLink* is a live-by-satellite evangelistic broadcast held in conjunction with home pizza parties. Churches and organizations often co-sponsor these, adding to the program in hopes of attracting more unsaved kids. *RIOTT* (Regina in Outreach to Teens) is a Canadian action-oriented theme party involving 50 churches, drawing hundreds of non-Christians and leading many of them to Christ. A *monthly evangelistic meeting* is led by students in Great Falls, Montana, and is co-sponsored by 15 churches. *Overtime* was a series of four after-game rallies in San Diego during October. One night they sponsored a cheer-leading competition between 12 schools—and 5,000 kids showed up!

Strategy. One goal of the Network is to be sure that there is a ministry to every campus by the year 2000. Target the campuses by obtaining a list of city schools and matching them with the names of youth workers you know are ministering there. In the San Francisco Bay area the Network prepared a *Profile* for each campus in all twelve school districts. In Mississippi, youth workers divided up the 360 high schools into 82 counties and 8 districts. In Portland, the 200 youth workers involved have adopted a mission statement: "Through a commitment to unity, concerted prayer and strategic cooperation, to provide the opportunity for every junior high and high school student to hear and respond to the Gospel of Jesus Christ by the year 2000."

Youth Worker Relationships.

At first this topic may not seem to fit well when addressing a subject like "cooperative evangelism." It certainly is not a program like many of those we've just mentioned. And yet, it is every bit as important—probably more important. Evangelism isn't really a program. In the spirit of Matthew's rendition of the Great Commission, it is something that happens "as you are going." It's a process that happens in the context of relationships. Therefore, it makes sense to take care of those leading the evangelism.

Many can plan programs for a few years and then burn out. But surrounding ourselves with quality relationships helps ensure that "after I have preached to others, I myself will not be disqualified . . ." (1 Cor 9:27).

Every Network member signs a covenant—part of it is a commitment to evangelism, but much of it is about accountability in other areas of our lives (e.g., personal holiness, home life). As we work together toward common goals, as we meet together month in and month out, we develop a bond which helps us persevere. Most groups have a monthly Network meeting where they share a meal and some casual conversation, interact over a topic of interest, talk about coming plans to cooperate, and conclude with a time of prayer.

Special times may be set aside to meet particular needs. The Network in Sacramento felt a need to focus on cultivating spiritual disciplines. So they arranged to spend part of a day at a Catholic monastery for the purpose of a special time alone with God--time for solitude, journaling, meditating on Scripture, praying and reflecting. The Network in the Northwest felt a need for a relational time with youth workers and spouses. So, they held a Rock 'n' Roll Rendezvous—two days of rock-climbing and river rafting—just for couples, no kids allowed.

A Network can also provide special retreats and conferences for spiritual nurture and refreshment. Or, they can tie into national and regional events like the annual Network Forums. Quite often, in that extended time away, the Lord has met with individuals in a life-changing way. On other occasions, the prayer times alone have served to re-kindle the fire for this lost generation. We have prayed together that every teenager would be exposed to the Gospel, that youth workers would cooperate without concern for who gets the credit, and that the youth culture would feel the impact of a new generation of young people who are boldly following Christ.

It's hard to come away from relational times like these without feeling encouraged to press on! In the process, most of us develop lasting relationships that serve not only as a network, but also as a "net"—something we can fall back on in time of need. In my own local Network, one of the members lost his month-old baby. He said to me after the funeral, "You just can't imagine the feelings I had when I looked out in the audience and saw one of the front rows filled with the guys from the Network."

The story is told of a young child lost in an African wilderness. Most of the the territory was covered with grass so tall that she could not be seen. The search did not begin until late in the afternoon, and though the family searched frantically, the small girl was not found by nightfall. In the sleepless night that followed, a plan was established and fellow-tribespeople were quick to volunteer their help. At dawn, instead of scattering in all directions as before, the group formed itself into a long line, joining hands. Methodically, they swept across the fields like a giant comb. In a short time, they found her—shivering with fright but alive.

This tribe had learned a valuable lesson which we also need to learn: we are much more effective working together than when we work separately. Their **purpose** was clear—they must save the child. They **organized leadership** based on their relationships. And they developed a **strategy** to meet the current need utilizing their available resources. This is what we must do if we are to reach the lost children around us—children just as vulnerable, due to the hostile environment in which they live.

With all due respect to the many things you are presently doing in your own ministry, I urge you to find a way to cooperate with others to reach the youth of your whole community for Christ. This is no time for provincialism. We must not squander the tremendous resources and momentum that put the fulfillment of the Great Commission within our grasp. Cooperating with believers is God's way of doing things. As we are obedient, I am convinced that we will be part of a movement of His Spirit that will sweep the world.

Eleven

Link Arms: Networking in Evangelism

Paul Fleischmann

Our ministry was seeing quite a bit of fruit in evangelism. We were focusing on schools in the Portland, Oregon, area, holding evangelistic outreach events and doing one-on-one evangelism. Lots of kids were coming to Christ—it was pretty exciting. But I kept hearing similar reports about another ministry across town. Something inside urged me to get together with this youth pastor, but for some reason I put it off. Finally, one day we arranged to have lunch. Frankly, I was nervous about it.

First impressions didn't really ease my insecurities. He was much more outgoing, athletic and charismatic than me. As he shared what they were doing to reach kids, I wasn't feeling excitement—I was feeling overwhelmed! And then, when he shared that his vision encompassed the whole city, I started to feel downright threatened! But, as my defense mechanisms started to kick in, something stopped my thinking process midstream. (As I look back, I am sure that "something" was really "Someone" who had placed a similar heart for the city in both of us!)

I started to see the pattern. We discovered that both of us wanted to see the whole city reached for Christ. Both of us had a vision that someday every school in the city would have a ministry, that youth leaders would be raised up to disciple students, that kids would be leading the way in personal evangelism. I remember asking, sort of sheepishly, "Do you think there are some ways we could work together?" He responding resoundingly, "Sure!!"

That was the beginning of a fruitful partnership. As it turned out, his efforts focused primarily on the west side of town, and mine focused most on the east side. At first, our "networking" was mainly through interaction and sharing ideas. Then I brought some leaders and a few students to some of his events. Before long we were working together on a few things and providing some interaction between our staff teams. Eventually, we co-sponsored an evangelistic winter retreat in the mountains. Many kids came to Christ, and a wonderful side effect was that our kids got to observe us working together. The result was that, in time, other youth workers caught the vision, and the first "Portland Network of Youth Ministries" was growing its roots.

A SHARED PURPOSE

It's great to have outstanding evangelistic events in your church or youth organization. But even though I hate to say it, that is not enough. The reason I hate to say it is that I know how hard you must be working already. I know how much work it takes to pull off a quality evangelistic event. I know how satisfying it is to see response when kids come to Christ from your efforts. I was experiencing all of this in my Portland ministry before I met with the youth pastor. But what we stumbled onto in Portland was something we all must come to grips with—God wants our whole city to know about Christ. He wants every teenager to be exposed to the Gospel.

The tendency, I've observed, is for us to "lose sight of the forest for the trees." We each have our own grove of trees that is our "Jerusalem" (Acts 1:8). It takes our total energy—and more! It is challenging, rewarding, frustrating, consuming, stretching. It is all that we can handle! We just can't try to take on the whole forest. This kind of thinking is understandable. It is our attempt to place limits, to be realistic, to guard our effectiveness by not taking on too much. But I wonder how it looks from God's perspective, looking down on "the forest" He created. I think He sees us, all too often, running into each other in the same grove of trees. In fact, there may be so much traffic in some areas that the trees may be actually sustaining some damage! At the same time, I think God sees huge areas of His forest with hardly any workers.

Haven't you seen that? In some cities, I know of three parachurch ministries and several churches all having active ministries on the same campus. Each has some justification as to why they should be there, yet there are other schools nearby without any ministry whatsoever. This is also true nationally. Some areas, like my own southern California, have hundreds of salaried youth workers. Other areas, like the northeast, have just a handful.

What should our response be? We can't just shrug our shoulders. We can't ignore the rest of the forest just because we are swamped, or because we'd prefer to minister elsewhere, or even because we are seeing results. When Jesus gave us the Great Commission to spread the Gospel to every person, it wasn't just a challenge, it was a command. It was *very important to Him*. Each Gospel closes with the Great Commission and the book of Acts opens with it! It is not enough for us to have an evangelism program in place. The point of the Great Commission is saturation with the Gospel—to every creature (Mark 16:15) in every nation (Matt. 28:19, Luke 24:47). Sure, we are called to our grove of trees, but we must minister there with a view to reaching the whole forest.

Imagine for a moment what would happen if we applied that limited strategy of local youth ministry to wartime. Each army would be fighting its own separate battles without a view to winning the war. The enemy might even accept the loss of a few battles, if he could sneak in unnoticed to capture vast areas while the opposing armies were "busy." We are also in a battle—more fierce than any human conflict—"against the rulers, against the authorities, against the powers of this dark world and against the spiritual forces of evil in the heavenly realms" (Eph. 6:12). It is a battle for the very souls of young people lost without Christ. We must not allow ourselves to be tricked by the enemy into thinking that the only battlefield that counts is the one where we are fighting. The commission of our Commander-in-Chief is to take the whole forest, and we must be sure that our local "campaign" is fitting in with His strategy to win the war on the larger scope.

A SHARED PLAN

You may be feeling a little overwhelmed right now. After all, the Great Commission is an overwhelming task! It's a "God-size" task which can be accomplished only by supernatural means. It can't be accomplished merely by working harder, getting more organized, exerting more influence, or any other trusted human approach. Fortunately, as a part of the Great Commission, Jesus promised that His authority and His presence would accompany His command (Matt 28:18-20). He would send His Holy Spirit to show us what to do on a daily basis (John 16:7-15). In fact, Jesus promised that we would be empowered to do the kinds of things that He did—and, "even greater things than these" (John 14:12)!

Since we are partners with the Holy Spirit, we must see our city through His eyes:

- What NEEDS does the Holy Spirit see in your community, as a whole?

- What RESOURCES does the Holy Spirit see in your community, as a whole?

- In light of the NEEDS and RESOURCES, what would the HOLY SPIRIT do to reach your community?

Two youth workers asked these questions of each other in Houston, Texas, several years ago. They dreamed of what God could do in their city. They met, talked, and prayed together for over two years. Finally, with the confirmation of a larger group of youth workers, they met to plan a city-wide evangelistic crusade called Something's Happening Houston. But it wasn't just another evangelistic event. Over 600 area churches became involved in using it as a tool for evangelism. The result was 6,000 youth in attendance each of three nights. In fact, the Spirit was moving so strongly that they felt led to "hold it over" an additional night—and 7,500 came! Over the 4 nights, 2,000 teenagers came to know Jesus as their Savior!

Since the Great Commission is Christ's command, the only hope we have to achieve it is by being careful to do it His way. In John 17, Christ poured out His heart to God about the world: "that all of them may be one, Father... so that the world may believe that you have sent me." Part of the reason that the youth workers in Houston made such an impact on their community was that they followed Christ's pattern for unity. But it is not some mystical method. It makes a tremendous amount of sense! Deuteronomy 32:30 states that, when empowered by God, "one man [can] chase a thousand or two [can] put ten thousand to flight." That's an increase of five hundred per cent in effectiveness by simply working together!

In modern terms, Webster calls that *synergy*: the combined action which yields greater results than the sum of the individual parts. An ancient idea applied recently to business is the concept of "leverage."

One person can lift far more than his weight if he positions his resources in such a way that his efforts are multiplied. In the military, we see this principle applied in the formation of alliances and joint operations. Allied forces scored notable triumphs in World War II and Operation Desert Storm.

One of the greatest privileges of my life has been to see this principle of oneness applied in reaching young people. It was just a simple idea, tried the year before on a single high school campus. Then in 1990, the Southern Baptists in Texas decided to try the idea within their denomination to get students to pray for the evangelism of their campus and community. They named it *See You at the Pole*. They could have kept the idea to themselves and still had a very successful program. But instead they shared the idea throughout the Texas Network, the state chapter of the National Network of Youth Ministries* which represents many denominations and youth organizations. To their amazement 45,000 teenagers from 1200 campuses gathered to pray before school. The idea spread like wildfire, and now each year *See You at the Pole* is observed by over a million young people in every state and in numerous other countries. A shared purpose based on a divine command is mobilizing a growing army of young troops for Christ!

A SHARED PARTNERSHIP

When people are working toward a shared purpose utilizing a shared plan, a wonderful sense of partnership develops. It doesn't always happen in that order. But it usually happens. And this is one of the most rewarding aspects of networking. Actually, it's pretty hard to have a real network without relationships, because networks are built on one crucial presupposition: **We need each other!** Paul characterizes the body of Christ in Ephesians 4:16 as one made up of those working in close relationship: "From Him the whole body joined and held together by every supporting ligament, grows and builds itself up in love, as each part does its work." Relationships happen in the process of heading in the same direction.

This is true in nature. Have you ever wondered why geese often fly in a "V" formation? Scientists have discovered that it's because they can fly 71 percent farther that way than when they fly alone. While heading in the same direction (shared purpose), they find that the "V" is an effective method (shared plan)—but only if they work in cooperation with each other (shared partnership). Imagine what would happen if they started competing with each other or going in different directions. In fact, they work in such oneness that the leadership changes often to give the lead goose a break (since it is taking the greatest wind resistance). And they look out for each other. If a goose becomes ill, gets shot by a hunter, or goes down for some other reason, two other geese go down with him for protection and care. I'm sure geese have their struggles in relationships just like humans do—they may be going efficiently in the same direction, but you always hear them honking loudly at each other!

Relationships can make the difference between making it and breaking it in ministry. I know from experience. During one of the roughest periods in my ministry I had started to lose perspective. It was then that I drew on the relationships I had with Barry St. Clair and another Network brother, Billy Beacham. When I asked for their insight they lovingly questioned me, challenged me, and prayed with me. But they spoke with the kind of candor and frankness that could have only come out of close relationship. It probably would have been too difficult to receive from someone I did not know as well. But because I knew Barry and Billy loved me, knew me well, and had my best interest at heart, I was able to accept their counsel. And the changes that resulted have affected my ministry to this day.

This is the kind of accountability that is much needed and yet sadly lacking in ministry today. A study conducted by Howard Hendricks of Dallas Theological Seminary reports that of 237 cases of moral failure in ministers, not one reported involvement in an accountability group. That is why it is so crucial to form a Network in your area. Working together for evangelism is one important aspect of the Network. But when that commitment is part of a covenant held in common by fellow members, there is more hope for lasting impact. Long after the event is over, the shared partnership will undergird you, sharpen you, and be a tool God can use in your life to keep you effective in evangelism for years to come.

"Two are better than one, because they have a
good return for their work.
If one falls down, his friend can help him up.
But pity the man who falls and has no one to help him up!
Though one may be overpowered, two can defend themselves.
A cord of three strands is not quickly broken."
(Ecclesiastes 4:9–10, 12)

159

For information about Network membership, contact
The National Network of Youth Ministries
17150 Via Del Campo, Suite 102
San Diego, CA 92127
Phone: 619-451-1111
FAX: 619-451-6900.

Twelve

Choose From the Options:
Deciding What Event to Do

Jim Burns

American businesses use the buzz word "reengineering" for the mid to late 1990s. When a business reengineers, it simply throws away the old ways of thinking and creates a fresh, new style of doing business. This is what I hope happens as you think about a city-wide outreach event. The excitement and synergy of big events make for powerful times in youth ministry. However, these events can become a time, financial and energy drain. To be perfectly honest, all of us have been part of events about which when said and done, we asked cynically, "Was it worth it?"

I remember when we put on an outreach concert at our church with one of the top Christian bands. Literally, I put in 100 hours on this one event. I stopped any other discipleship programming for a couple of weeks so my youth workers and I could put in the hours to recruit students to the outreach event. The evening was exciting as 2,500 students filled our auditorium. The reason for the event was outreach for our church. Yet the next Sunday we had a "big zero" of new kids in the youth group meeting and half of my volunteer staff didn't show up because they were burned out from all the work of the outreach concert. We spent half our year's budget, canceled other less flashy events, and physically and emotionally wiped out. Did we reach our goals of outreach? I must admit that I wish I could take back those hundreds of hours of work and the thousands of dollars it cost us. With the same amount of money I could have hired an intern to work on a campus all year. With the hundreds of "man and woman hours" we could have invested a great amount of discipleship time which would have definitely produced more spiritual fruit. This doesn't mean all big events will drain us, but it does mean we have to look very carefully at how to best facilitate them.

In light of that we want to ask seriously, "What real fruit will come out of this?" With the application of the first nine chapters to your present choice of a big event, I'm happy to say "fruit—more fruit—much more fruit" (John 15:1-16).

With all of the resources available to you today, you seldom have to drown in the creation and implementation of a city-wide outreach event. The purpose of this chapter is to give you creative options that will keep you from doing that.

With a view to "reengineering" your approach, here are some choices you can make that will not wipe you out, but instead produce "fruit that remains."

CREATE IT

Although it takes more time, there is nothing quite like a fresh new idea. A youth worker network works beautifully when you put several youth workers together around a table and start brainstorming ideas for an event. Usually you come up with a terrific plan. One group we know came up with a "Raw Chicken Festival." They had each student bring a raw chicken as their entry into the event. There were awards for the "best dressed" chicken, bathing suit contest, talent show with chickens, and several relays including a wheelbarrow race. For dinner they had barbecued chicken! It took a group of youth workers several cups of coffee around a breakfast one morning to come up with the idea. They say (I didn't go, I'm allergic to chicken) that it was the most successful outreach of the year.

Of course you don't have to create something as bizarre as a "raw chicken festival." Creating an event has positive value because people tend to *support what they create*.

HIRE IT

Today you can hire many ready-made events. Many organizations do custom ready-made events. They come with the program, flyers, and directions. For a fee, you know you have a proven product. The same goes for bringing in a musician, band or speaker. In a sense, you hire the talent and the program without having to create it. When you hire it, you will know what you get; that is, unless you haven't previewed the talent. And not previewing talent is the number one mistake when you hire for an event. If it's impossible to preview the talent or program, then ask for the phone numbers of several people who have hired them before you.

RENT IT

Sometimes renting is much more economical then buying. The same goes with events. In today's world it's better to rent the film rather than buy it. Rent the ice skating rink and have your city-wide ice broom hockey competition. Almost every fun center is for rent to large groups. I know one group who rented an entire carnival with a live elephant ride as well. You can take over miniature golf courses, swimming pools, gymnasiums, malls, theaters—the list could go on and on. A youth workers' network in San Diego once rented Sea World and packed it with 5,000 students for an outreach event.

BORROW IT

Here's a phrase worth remembering in youth ministry: "The essence of creativity is the ability to copy." I'm not talking about plagiarism, I just mean copying. If a network of youth workers is doing some great city-wide outreach in Charlotte, why shouldn't members of a group from Orlando borrow the idea and try it in their city? If you attended a large denominational event and it was a smashing success, then take the ideas that worked back home. I know of a youth worker who attended a big event where the stage design was outstanding. When the event was over he asked the leadership what they planned to do with the stage. They said, "Use it for fire wood." He took it home and it became the stage for a youth rally he had planned several weeks later. Some people have borrowed excellently-produced video scenes from other large events.

Sometimes you can even borrow the speaker or musician. For example, some youth workers in Alabama heard I was going to be speaking at a convention in Atlanta. Six months before the event they "piggy backed" that event and asked me to fly into Montgomery, Alabama, a day early for a city-wide rally. It worked for them. The Atlanta convention was paying for the majority of airfare and my honorarium. They fed me some good Southern country food and handed me a much smaller check than I received in Atlanta, but I was very pleased to do two events instead of one.

If you can borrow ideas or things from others, you may save yourself a ton of time and money.

JOIN IT

Perhaps one of the most effective ways to do a big event is to join one already in existence. When Amy Grant comes to town, make it a big deal with your group, buy the tickets, take a bus to the concert together, and let Amy (or whoever) minister to your kids. You don't have to create the event, but you can attend a quality event with very little responsibility on your part.

Who likes to do logistics? Most of us would rather spend our time in ministry with kids rather than ticket sales. Today several organizations plan regional and national events that you can join. They offer the finest in programming, publicity and follow up. Take advantage of somebody else's putting on the event and bring your students to a quality event without the hassles of making it your responsibility.

No one option is better than another. Find the option that fits your needs and go for it. If you stay in youth work very long you will end up trying all of these options.

CREATIVE OUTREACH EVENT IDEAS

1. **Concert.** Since music is the medium for students today, a concert can bring kids to an event more effectively than probably any other source.

2. **Comedy.** The secular world has definitely gone crazy for comedy. Why not use good clean comedy as a tool to reach students?

3. **Drama.** A well done play is most often much more effective than a speaker.

4. **Speaker.** The world still loves an outstanding communicator.

5. **Run for Hungry Children (5K/10K).** Who says an event has to happen in an auditorium? I know a yearly event that raises thousands of dollars

for Christian relief agencies, brings the community together for a run, and provides a great evangelistic outreach to the community.

6. **Car Rally.** They're coming back. Kids love 'em. When the car part of the rally is over you can have a program at a church, gym, pizza parlor, or wherever.

7. **Film.** Putting on a big event with a film allows you to monitor the quality of the film and the discussion afterwards.

8. **College Fair.** Many college admissions departments would love to help you put on a college fair. Students from all over your city come to it out of a desire to learn more about schools, scholarships, and tuition. You can even have a short program geared around the Gospel before they browse around the fair.

9. **Walk for Life.** Many cities have set up "walk-for-life" days where students take a stand for life issues. Other walk-for-life programs help raise funds through sponsorship for a needed crisis pregnancy center or drug rehabilitation center. You can creatively share Christ in an event like this.

10. **Overtime/5th Quarter.** This event capitalizes on kids' enthusiasm after a football game or other school event. Use the school, a gym or auditorium. Good food and a brief, powerful presentation of the Gospel make a dynamite combination.

11. **Breakfast Outreach.** Using a professional athlete to speak or a special musician, youth leaders challenge students to come and bring their friends.

12. **Television/Radio Special.** With the addition of cable it's now quite economical, and even free in some markets, to produce television and radio special events.

13. **Sports Competition.** Athletes are still a huge draw. Many cities have successfully pulled off outreach events based on volleyball, basketball, softball and other sports celebrities and tournaments.

14. **Compassion Project.** Compassion International has a wonderful free program to help put together an event that can promote hunger relief and support for Third World relief needs. The videos, cassettes, and curriculum are all free. Instantly this has great potential for evangelism.

15. **Let It Growl.** This is World Vision's hunger awareness program for students. It's filled with great ideas and it helps students look beyond themselves. Non-Christians will be intrigued by the challenge.

16. **School Assemblies.** You want to do a big outreach event? Why not hook up with your local school and bring in a top communicator or assembly program? You have a huge ready-made audience. Many churches will then use the communicator that evening for a Christ-centered outreach. It's a winner.

17. **"The Door."** We know of several churches who sponsor a recreation center, coffee house, or just open up the church on weekends. The reason we named it "The Door" is because almost half the centers we know about are called "The Door." It's a great name for an evangelical event!

Thirteen

Get in the Flow:
Working Smarter Not Harder

Jim Burns

A flow chart is a device which you follow in order to ensure that things get done for your outreach event. It is meant to be thorough, detailed, and easy to follow.

The National Institute of Youth Ministry sponsors a city-wide youth event called THIS SIDE UP (TSU). It's an experience that encompasses more than just a one-day event. THIS SIDE UP focuses on a city-wide rally. However, to get there, we precede it with youth worker training, luncheons, parent forums and student peer leadership training. Then we follow up with a post TSU youth event. It's big like the proverbial elephant. So that we enjoy it, we eat it one bite at a time. We have prepared some very practical utensils to help us do that.

THE HARD QUESTION CHART

When you meet to determine whether or not to take the challenge of doing a big city-wide event, you will need to ask yourself several significant questions. Don't be satisfied with easy answers! When these questions are answered thoroughly *in writing*, then you know that God's hand is in it.

Why?

Why do you want to put on an outreach event? This can become a time-consuming energy drain. Are your motives right? Is your purpose clear? Without a clear-cut purpose statement that everyone understands, you can easily lose focus.

A purpose statement example:

Great Adventure exists to present the Gospel clearly and relevantly to non-Christian youth with an opportunity for them to respond to the call to become Christians.

Who?

The "Who" question moves you to the next level. Who will be involved? Who will commit to leadership? Who will pray and work to make this event a success? Youth workers get excited about the idea of a big outreach event, but it's one of the first responsibilities they drop when they get too busy. Who, among your leaders, is strongly committed to give time, energy, focus, prayer and finances?

What?

What will the event look like and what will it take to make it happen (logistics)? One of the problems in answering the "what" question is that youth workers tend to create too elaborate an event. Sure, it would be great to have Josh McDowell shoot out of a cannon, along with a Beatles reunion tour and a personal visit from the last 10 Miss Americas. Let's get down to reality. It is good to ask ourselves, "Are we building an elaborate Ferrari when all we really need and can afford is a Jeep?"

Where?

Where will the event take place? You will have to answer this when you have a rough estimate about how many will attend. A church facility is usually the cheapest. A school auditorium, convention center, or football field is more neutral. When you determine if you will have food, games, music, video, then you'll be able to make wise decisions about the facility. We've found that the cost of the event will also often determine where the event will be held.

When?

The time of year and other events will help determine the "when" of your event. Keep this principle in mind: the more students expected to attend, the longer it takes to plan the event. Don't set a date until you've realistically worked out your flow chart. (See the Outreach Event Planner.)

How much?

Over and over again budgeting gets neglected in a big event. Many let their enthusiasm and creativity bounce off the walls in designing big events, but few have the foresight to ask: "So how much is this going to cost, and who's going to pay for it?" Every youth speaker and Christian musician I know has participated in at least one large, successful, "fruitful" event only to have the sponsor of the event say, "It was great but we lost our shirts financially. Would you be willing to take less honorarium or no honorarium at all?" Our suggestion is to get financial commitments ahead of time to pay for the event. That way you can deal with lower attendance and not worry about finances. Some large event programmers suggest that for the best financial and people response, ask a specific number of churches to sign a contract on a minimum number of attendees to the event. When you know how much they will commit, then toy can set and follow your budget. The following page will help you answer these crucial questions for your city-wide outreach event.

City-Wide Event "Hard Questions"

City-Wide Event Idea:

Why?

Who?

What?

Where?

When?

How Much?

THE "FLOW" CHART

Every outreach event needs a flow chart. I've included one that covers most of the details of any outreach event, but obviously you will need to create and adapt to meet your needs.

Weeks out from event	Date Completed	Person in Charge	
			BUDGET
____	____	____	Projections complete
____	____	____	Approval from the network planning team
____	____	____	Commitments/pledges made
____	____	____	Final working budget complete
			DATES
____	____	____	Review options for dates
____	____	____	Approval from network planning team
____	____	____	Select final dates
			PROGRAM
____	____	____	Develop concept and theme options
____	____	____	Design story boards to present
____	____	____	Approval from network planning team
____	____	____	Final choice selected
			FACILITY
____	____	____	Review options for facilities
____	____	____	Final facilities selected
____	____	____	Contact facility for availability on date
____	____	____	Pencil in date
____	____	____	Discuss fees
____	____	____	Finalize fees and date
____	____	____	Requested contract
____	____	____	Maps requested
____	____	____	Contract received
____	____	____	Maps received
____	____	____	Check request for deposit submitted
____	____	____	Review contract
____	____	____	Deposit sent
____	____	____	Final contract returned
			MUSIC
____	____	____	Review options for musicians
____	____	____	Approval from network planning team
____	____	____	Final choice selected
____	____	____	Contact musician or manager for availability on date
____	____	____	Discuss fees
____	____	____	Pencil in date
____	____	____	Finalize fees and date
____	____	____	Requested contract
____	____	____	Promo materials requested

——— ——— ——— Contract received
——— ——— ——— Promo materials received
——— ——— ——— Check request for deposit submitted
——— ——— ——— Review contract
——— ——— ——— Deposit sent
——— ——— ——— Final contract returned
——— ——— ——— Purpose statement sent
——— ——— ——— Prayer letter sent
——— ——— ——— Outline of program sent

SPEAKER–Keynote
——— ——— ——— Review options for speakers
——— ——— ——— Approval from network planning team
——— ——— ——— Final choice selected
——— ——— ——— Contact speaker or manager for
availability on date
——— ——— ——— Discuss fees
——— ——— ——— Pencil in date
——— ——— ——— Finalize fees and date
——— ——— ——— Requested contract
——— ——— ——— Promo materials requested
——— ——— ——— Contract received
——— ——— ——— Promo materials received
——— ——— ——— Check request for deposit submitted
——— ——— ——— Review contract
——— ——— ——— Deposit sent
——— ——— ——— Final contract returned
——— ——— ——— Purpose statement sent
——— ——— ——— Prayer letter sent
——— ——— ——— Outline of program sent

MUSIC–Worship Leader
——— ——— ——— Review options for musicians
——— ——— ——— Approval from network planning team
——— ——— ——— Final choice selected
——— ——— ——— Contact musician or manager for
availability on date
——— ——— ——— Discuss fees
——— ——— ——— Pencil in date
——— ——— ——— Finalize fees and date
——— ——— ——— Requested contract
——— ——— ——— Promo materials requested
——— ——— ——— Contract received
——— ——— ——— Promo materials received
——— ——— ——— Check request for deposit submitted
——— ——— ——— Review contract
——— ——— ——— Deposit sent
——— ——— ——— Final contract returned
——— ——— ——— Purpose statement sent
——— ——— ——— Prayer letter sent

____	____	____	Outline of program sent

TESTIMONIES

____	____	____	Review options for testimonies
____	____	____	Approval from network planning team
____	____	____	Final choices selected
____	____	____	Contact for availability on date
____	____	____	Discuss fees
____	____	____	Pencil in date
____	____	____	Finalize fees and date
____	____	____	Requested contract
____	____	____	Promo materials requested
____	____	____	Contract received
____	____	____	Promo materials received
____	____	____	Check request for deposit submitted
____	____	____	Review contract
____	____	____	Deposit sent
____	____	____	Final contract returned
____	____	____	Purpose statement sent
____	____	____	Prayer letter sent
____	____	____	Outline of program sent

COMEDY AND/OR DRAMA

____	____	____	Review options for comedy/drama
____	____	____	Approval from network planning team
____	____	____	Final choice selected
____	____	____	Contact speaker or manager for availability on date
____	____	____	Discuss fees
____	____	____	Pencil in date
____	____	____	Finalize fees and date
____	____	____	Requested contract
____	____	____	Promo materials requested
____	____	____	Contract received
____	____	____	Promo materials received
____	____	____	Check request for deposit submitted
____	____	____	Review contract
____	____	____	Deposit sent
____	____	____	Final contract returned
____	____	____	Purpose statement sent
____	____	____	Prayer letter sent
____	____	____	Outline of program sent

MARKETING/MAILINGS

(Announcing Upcoming Dates)

____	____	____	Design layout options
____	____	____	Design story boards to present
____	____	____	Approval from network planning team
____	____	____	Final choice selected
____	____	____	Research printers and payment plans

—— —— —— Receive quotes
—— —— —— Finalize printer
—— —— —— Order mailing list
—— —— —— Finalize roughs
—— —— —— Deliver to printer
—— —— —— Request check for printer
—— —— —— Printer paid
—— —— —— Deliver to mailhouse
—— —— —— Request check for postage
—— —— —— Deliver to postmaster
—— —— —— Postmaster paid

YOUTH WORKER LUNCHEONS

—— —— —— Select three regional dates
—— —— —— Contact facilities for availability on date
—— —— —— Pencil in date
—— —— —— Discuss fees
—— —— —— Finalize fees and date
—— —— —— Request contract
—— —— —— Contract received
—— —— —— Check request for deposit submitted
—— —— —— Review contract
—— —— —— Deposit sent
—— —— —— Final contract returned
—— —— —— Maps requested
—— —— —— Maps received
—— —— —— Design promotional material to hand out
—— —— —— Secure volunteers for event
—— —— —— Send thank-you letter to facility
—— —— —— Send follow-up letter to attendees

PROMO VIDEO

—— —— —— Design concept and theme
—— —— —— Approval from network planning team
—— —— —— Research producers
—— —— —— Set date to produce
—— —— —— Order tapes for luncheons and registration

T-SHIRTS

—— —— —— Design story boards to present
—— —— —— Approval from staff and management team
—— —— —— Final choice selected
—— —— —— Research printers
—— —— —— Order shirts for luncheon and

preregistration packets

PROFESSIONAL COUNSELORS

—— —— —— Prepare list of ministries to approach to

coordinate

—— —— —— Prepare job description involved

____ ____ ____ Prepare letter to send
____ ____ ____ Follow up on letter
____ ____ ____ Finalize ministry to coordinate

COORDINATORS AND VOLUNTEERS

____ ____ ____ Prepare list of names for volunteer coordinator
____ ____ ____ Finalize volunteer coordinator
____ ____ ____ Prepare list of names for key coordinator positions
____ ____ ____ Prepare job description and responsibility
____ ____ ____ Call through list and see who is interested
____ ____ ____ Finalize all coordinators
____ ____ ____ Prepare letter for past volunteers
____ ____ ____ Merge letter and stuff
____ ____ ____ Request postmaster check
____ ____ ____ Letters delivered to postmaster
____ ____ ____ Volunteer response letter prepared
____ ____ ____ Follow up on potential volunteers w/phone campaign
____ ____ ____ Finalize all volunteers
____ ____ ____ Send out confirmation letter w/maps to volunteers
____ ____ ____ Meet with coordinators on phone or at facility
____ ____ ____ Send thank-you letter w/evaluation

PRAYER

____ ____ ____ Secure coordinator
____ ____ ____ Schedule date for prayer dessert
____ ____ ____ Prepare letter w/invitation
____ ____ ____ Send letter out
____ ____ ____ Prepare prayer letter for speakers, musicians and coordinators
____ ____ ____ Send out letter

PHONE CAMPAIGN

____ ____ ____ Prepare list of names
____ ____ ____ Select date for all-day calling event
____ ____ ____ Find volunteers or staff to make calls
____ ____ ____ Prepare materials to send out
____ ____ ____ Update notes and results in computer

PROGRAM GUIDE

____ ____ ____ Design layout options
____ ____ ____ Design story boards to present
____ ____ ____ Approval from network planning team
____ ____ ____ Final choice selected
____ ____ ____ Research printers and payment plans

___	___	___
___	___	___

____ ____ ____ Receive quotes
____ ____ ____ Finalize printer
____ ____ ____ Finalize roughs
____ ____ ____ Deliver to printer
____ ____ ____ Request check for printer
____ ____ ____ Printer paid

STAGE
____ ____ ____ Design layout options
____ ____ ____ Design story boards to present
____ ____ ____ Approval from network planning team
____ ____ ____ Final choice selected
____ ____ ____ Acquire props and build

SIGNS
____ ____ ____ Design layout options
____ ____ ____ Design story boards to present
____ ____ ____ Final choice selected
____ ____ ____ Acquire props and build

Pretty interesting reading, huh? Obviously it's meant to save you and your network hours of work.

THE TIME LINE

After you have put together a flow chart, you will want to make a time line. The time line keeps everyone involved accountable. It measures the success of the preprogramming side of an outreach event. Creating a time line is as simple as taking the dates on your flow chart and putting them on a master calendar. Then everyone knows when every detail is due to be completed.

THE PUBLICITY PUSH

Your publicity is only as good as the motivation of the groups and the individual kids who are coming. The youth leader's ability to challenge his kids, and the kids' desire to take the challenge, makes or breaks the event. All other publicity creates awareness and keeps the level of motivation high. Most youth leaders are born salesmen, but publicizing city-wide outreach events takes extra effort. Consider the following sources for advertising your event.

- Church bulletins and newsletters
- Youth events already on the calendar
- Youth worker training seminars
- Youth Ministry Networks
- Mailings
- Radio
- Television
- Promo video

- Parachurch organizations
- T-shirts, stickers, buttons, etc.
- Denominational groups and publications
- Schools (kids give out tickets or flyers to friends)
- Phone calls
- Speaking opportunities

You have more ideas here than you can use, but out of these you can choose the ones that fit your event best. Create a plan that will bring students to the event and guarantee that the attendance will be a success.

THE "V" FACTOR

Volunteers! You must have them. When you create a city-wide outreach event you will need more volunteers than you ever imagined. It's a huge task to recruit and manage the volunteers. You will need job descriptions and flow charts whenever possible. Decide from this practical list of possible jobs for volunteers which ones you need. Put people together in teams for accountability and synergy.

- Audio/visual
- Brochure
- Facility
- Phone calls
- Program/Speakers/Musicians
- Registration
- Youth Worker's meetings
- Budget
- Crowd management
- On-site administration
- Prayer
- Publicity
- Security
- Stage

You don't want to make the task of writing volunteer job descriptions overwhelming, but you'll find it much better to have clearly-defined, brief descriptions for each task. If you aren't the administrative type, then recruit someone who likes to write job descriptions and manage this. There are people who actually love doing those tasks! Here are some sample job descriptions to get you started.

JOB DESCRIPTION: **PEER COUNSELING TRAINING COORDINATOR**

REPORTS TO: **EVENTS DIRECTOR**

On July 8th, we will have approximately 1,000 young people and youth leaders who will be equipped to handle the large number of individuals who come forward.

In order that the Peer Counselors may be prepared and equipped on-site, we will need to spend several hours training them. The training will be three-phase: evangelism, referral, and logistics. The training coordinator will be responsible for the following:

- Research and develop the evangelism aspect of training.

- Assist in direction of overall training, including recruitment and acquisition of volunteers and team leaders.

- Assist in all aspects of training program, including program schedule and curriculum.

- Oversee Peer Counseling movement and logistics on July 8th.

- Maintain contact with Peer Counselor Foremen throughout May/June to maintain enthusiasm for Peer Counseling.

- Maintain information flow to event director.

Time Requirement: 2-4 hours per week March–July

JOB DESCRIPTION: **PEER COUNSELING TRAINING FOREMEN**

REPORT TO: **PEER COUNSELING TRAINING COORDINATOR**

The Peer Counseling Training Foremen will oversee 10-12 individual Peer and Adult Counselors before and during THIS SIDE UP.
Responsibilities include:

- Attend at least one of the Peer Counseling Training Programs offered 4/29 and 5/13.

- Make frequent and consistent telephone contact with team members during subsequent weeks leading up to THIS SIDE UP.

- Hold at least one refresher/update meeting within two weeks of THIS SIDE UP.

- Shift Peer Counselors as necessary to accommodate those making new decisions on July 8.

Time Requirement: 4-6 hours per week through June.

JOB DESCRIPTION: PEER COUNSELORS/ADULT LEADER

REPORTS TO: PEER COUNSELORS FOREMEN

Peer Counselors and Adult Leaders will do the actual counseling and ministry in the counseling center. Their responsibilities include:

- Purchase an advanced pass to THIS SIDE UP ($12.50)
- Attend one of the Peer Counseling Training Programs offered 4/29 and 5/13.
- Complete memory verses and make frequent reviews of materials prior to THIS SIDE UP.
- Attend any of the follow-up meetings pulled together by your foreman.
- Arrive early on July 8th for final instructions.
- Lead peers coming for counseling to Christ.
- Make referrals when necessary.

Time Requirement: 6 hours of training; participation at THIS SIDE UP.

THE BIG BAD BUDGET

It's almost ironic that I am mentioning budget, since during my first year of youth ministry I went over budget in March! However, I've learned the hard way that the only way to have a successful event with less stress is to create a budget, follow the budget, and be accountable to it. My suggestion is that you find an "accountant type" to help manage and create your budget.

Listed below is a sample of offerings in an outreach budget. Again, this is meant only as an illustration of something you can adapt for your own event.

INCOME	PROJECTION
Registration	$90,000.00
Exhibitor	$6,000.00
Arts	$4,000.00
Dinner Sales	$8,000.00
T-shirts	$9,000.00
Tape Sales	$1,500.00
Resources/Concessions	
Subtotal	
DISBURSEMENTS	
Audio/Visual	$17,500.00
—sound	
—video	
—lighting	
—camera operator	
—producer	
—miscellaneous	
—opening video	
—airplane	
—radios	
—stage	
Subtotal	

INCOME	PROJECTION
FACILITY	$6,300.00
–facility rental	
–facility misc.	
–facility staff	
–equipment rental	
–exhibit linens	
–signage	
Subtotal	
HONORARIUMS	$17,000.00
–speakers	
–workshops	
–musicians	
Subtotal	
PRE-EVENTS	$5,000.00
–luncheon	
–counselor training	
–youth worker meetings	
Subtotal	
MISCELLANEOUS	$46,650.00
–marketing	
–media	
–promo video	
–postage (bulk)	
–hospitality	
–lodging	
–in-n-out/drinks	
–printing	
–program guides	
–program ent.	

INCOME	PROJECTION
Miscellaneous (cont.)	
–shipping	
–travel (staff and artist)	
–T-shirts	
–truck rental	
–wristbands	
–misc.	
–stationary	
–office supplies	
–UPS	
Subtotal	
MARKETING	
–YW mailings	
–brochure (print)	$3,800.00
–brochure (design)	$800.00
–mail house fees	$3,482.00
–mailing list	$375.00
–postage	$4,580.00
Subtotal	
TOTAL	
NET PROFIT	

Conclusion: This "nitty-gritty" information will cause you to focus. Once you have focused your purpose and know what you want to do, you can then flow with the chart, job description and budget that will keep you on track. As you all work hard together not only will you build a "team" of youth leaders in your city, but you will move closer to leading every kid on every campus in your community!

– PART 3 –

THE OUTREACH EVENT PLANNER

> Photocopy multiple copies of this material to use
> in your ongoing planning for outreach events.

Some pages of "The Outreach Event Planner" were adapted from materials used by permission of Student Impact, Willow Creek Community Church, 67 East Algonquin Road, South Barrington, IL 60010; (708) 382-6200. My thanks to Bo Boshears.

MY BURDEN FOR KIDS*

Write down what God gives you as a burden for lost kids.

1. How God wants me to see them

2. How God wants me to seek them

*See Chapter 1 of *The Magnet Effect* for content.

PURPOSE STATEMENT*

Write your purpose statement, then go over it with two trusted friends. When you get it in its final form, prepare it for presentation to others.

*See Chapter 2 of *The Magnet Effect* for content.

FIVE ESSENTIALS FOR EXCELLENCE*

Once you have watched the strategy video, fill out this sheet. Write down what you plan to do to implement the five essentials. Be specific.

1. Living under the Lordship of Christ

2. Building a leadership team of volunteers

3. Discipling students for maturity and ministry

4. Penetrating the campus through relationships

5. Designing outreach events to draw kids to Christ

*See Chapter 3 of *The Magnet Effect* for content.

REACH OUT STRATEGY RESOURCES

Committed Adult Leaders

Reach Out Strategy Videos, a 6-part video series, will inspire vision for a practical strategy in youth leaders. No. 8-7640 **$19.99**

Building Leaders for Strategic Youth Ministry brings together an adult ministry team, equips them spiritually, challenges them with a vision, and gives them practical tools to minister to kids. No. 6-1288 **$12.99**

Motivated Student Disciples

The Moving Toward Maturity Series offers a progressive, 5-level discipleship opportunity that will move kids from where they are to spiritual leadership in the youth group and in their schools.

Following Jesus lays the foundation for a strong relationship with Christ. No. 6-1290 **$5.99**

Spending Time Alone With God helps teens develop communication with Christ through a meaningful, consistent devotional life. No. 6-1292 **$5.99**

Time Alone With God Notebook guides students through a simple plan of daily prayer and Bible study. No. 6-3143 **$4.99**

Making Jesus Lord helps kids discover the wonders of Jesus and how to obey Him in the difficult issues they face everyday. No. 6-1293 **$5.99**

Giving Away Your Faith creates desire and ability in students to share Christ with their friends. No. 6-1297 **$5.99**

Influencing Your World challenges students to become servant leaders in the church and at school. No. 6-1294 **$5.99**

Moving Toward Maturity Leader's Guide provides everything needed to successfully lead the discipleship group. No. 6-1298 **$9.99**

Relational Outreach

The Facts of Life is a tool designed for kids to share Christ with their friends. No. 6-3141 **25 for $8.75**

Getting Started begins a new believer in a solid relationship with Christ. No. 6-3142 **$1.99**

Penetrating the Campus helps leaders develop a campus ministry to reach students where they are. No. 6-3085 **$8.99**

Taking Your Campus for Christ shows teens how to reach the campus by radically loving their friends. No. 6-3201 **$4.99**

The Magnet Effect Video shows youth leaders what an outreach event looks like and how to put one together.

To Order, Call *Reach Out Ministries*: (404) 441-2247
or call your local Christian bookstore.

A SAMPLE VISION AND STRATEGY STATEMENT

PHILOSOPHY AND STRATEGY OF YOUTH MINISTRY FOR

(name of your church)

Young people today are in crisis.

- 3.3 million of 17 million teens are alcoholics.
- 1 in 5 twelfth graders have tried crack or cocaine.
- 1/2 of the one-million teenage pregnancies end in abortion.
- Three times as many teenagers will commit suicide this year as the number of Americans killed at Pearl Harbor.

These negative statistics and others that are just as painful have names and faces. Many of them live in our community and go to our schools.

God has commissioned us to **GO** and reach these young people with the love and life-changing message of Jesus Christ. As well, He has commanded us to give them an opportunity to **GROW** in the fellowship of a local church. The Lord has called us to produce in these kids *life-change* and them help them become *life-changers.*

YOUTH MINISTRY MISSION STATEMENT

As Jesus Christ releases his life through us, we will GO to young people with the life-changing message of Christ and help them GROW to become life-changers to their friends.

In order to do this, our church must have a practical, biblical strategy of youth ministry. That means that every goal of the youth ministry must come out of principles of Scripture and find expression in practical programs. The **goals** we pursue will cause us to fulfill our mission statement.

To provide positive role models for our young people.

As I, the youth pastor, the adult leaders, and parents live under the Lordship of Jesus Christ, then our teenagers will have the opportunity to see the reality of Jesus Christ worked out in practical obedience and practical living. As we are experiencing God, they will experience God. That works itself out through

- confessing and repenting of sin regularly
- making any wrong relationships right

- obeying Christ fully and completely
- praying for the young people

To build a leadership team to minister to young people.

God has called some people specifically to work with young people. These adults need encouragement and equipping in order to have an effective ministry. We will nurture them in their commitment to Christ, encourage them in their relationships with other youth leaders, and train them in the skills they need to work with teenagers. They will learn how to express the life of Christ to kids. This will happen through a weekly Leadership Team gathering.

To motivate young people to experience life-change and become life-changers.

Many young people are not motivated by Jesus Christ. We want Him to be their life. To accomplish that, we must do with them what Jesus did with his disciples—disciple them. In an environment of total acceptance and personal relationships, we will help kids experience Christ, grow in Him, and then give that faith away to their friends. They will progress through five levels of growth.

1. *Following Jesus.* They will grasp the basics of knowing Jesus and following Him.

2. *Spending Time Alone with God.* They will learn and then experience how to have a daily time with God in the Bible and in prayer.

3. *Making Jesus Lord.* Looking at their felt needs like acceptance, friendships, and dating, they will learn how the Father, Son, and Holy Spirit relate to their lives practically.

4. *Giving Away Their Faith.* Seeing their friends through God's eyes, they will learn how to radically love their friends and express their faith to them.

5. *Influencing Their World.* As they learn what the Bible says about serving others, they will experience it practically as they serve their friends in the cafeteria, serve "the least" in the community, and catch God's heart for the entire world.

In this process they will move toward maturity.

To penetrate the campus.

The campus is the most challenging mission field in America today. It is a hostile, pressure-packed battle zone. Young people spend most of their time on the campus. Every day they face overwhelming emotional, social, and spiritual challenges. We need to reach them where they are. We will train and mobilize lay people and college students to build relationships with non-Christian young people in order to lead them to Christ. As adults do this, then our core of young people will have the courage to follow in our footsteps and boldly share Christ with their friends.

To design outreach events that draw kids to Christ.

Non-Christian kids need Jesus Christ. They need a place to come, hear the message of Christ, and respond to it. Christian kids need to feel comfortable bringing their friends. Therefore, we desire to creatively present the message of Christ to young people in a culturally relevant, enthusiastic, large group meeting. These events require intensive labor, much preparation, and the involvement of the church. We will follow a step-by-step plan to reach kids through these outreach events.

As we accomplish these goals, we will fulfill our Youth Ministry Mission Statement. Then in time and in cooperation with other churches, we will be able **to reach every kid on every campus in our community!**

OUTREACH EVENT SAMPLE BUDGET (WEEKLY)

1.	Publicity	$100
2.	Visual Media	$100
3.	Follow-up and Meeting Materials	$50
4.	Food	$50
5.	Speaker Honorarium/Music	$100
	TOTAL	$400

Your own budget will vary depending on the size of your youth group.

YOUTH MINISTRY PRAYER STRATEGY*

My personal strategy

Leaders' strategy

Students' strategy

*See Chapter 4 of *The Magnet Effect* for content.

OUTREACH EVENTS READINESS ASSESSMENT*

Category	Momentum now	Actions for total momentum
THE LEADER		
Philosophy clearly defined		
Vision expanded		
Ownership with leaders and students		
Evangelism modeled consistently		
THE PASTOR AND CHURCH LEADERSHIP		
Leadership prayed for		
Vision presented		
Church has counted cost		
Relevancy issue addressed		
Specific support secured		
Leaders invited to attend		
THE LEADERSHIP TEAM		
Leaders relating to non-Christians		
Leaders' roles communicated		
THE STUDENT TEAM		
Students equipped in evangelism		
Students challenged to ownership and responsibility		

*See Chapter 5 in *The Magnet Effect* for content.

192

PUBLICITY PLAN*

The plan to create a witness awareness in my youth group:

The plan to practically equip students to share Christ and bring their friends:
To build love and openness

To develop social skills

To train to witness

The plan for publicizing the event:
Changed lives. Who are they?

Discipleship groups. Who will they bring?

*See Chapter 6 of *The Magnet Effect* for content.

The youth group. What specific approach will we use?

Leadership team. Who do they invite?

Structured outreach. How will we organize it?

Telephone survey. How will we organize it?

Campus publicity. What will we use and how?

- Posters.
- Tracts.
- School paper.
- Public address announcements.
- Fliers.
- Mailings.
- Special group invitations.
- Advertisements.
- Youth hangouts.
- Local newspapers.
- Radio and television.

A SAMPLE PRESS RELEASE
(Your Logo)

(Address)

For Immediate Release

(Date)

"The youth of America are desperate," says a local church youth worker, and that includes students in Toledo.

Jeff Hankson, the youth minister at Toledo Community Church, says, "More than 5,000 teenagers commit suicide each year. Out of the one millions girls who will get pregnant this year, roughly 800,000 will be unmarried. And the statistics like these go on and on, covering every area: abortion, drinking, alcoholism, drugs, violence, and the occult."

"We can't close our eyes to these statistics, because they point to real problems for real kids here in our own town," he said.

Rather than launch into a tirade against these problems from a pulpit, Hankson and his church have developed a program and committed $32,500 this year to help area youth. Specific events planned for this year include a Christian music concert at Hensley Park, a week-long summer retreat, small groups for support, a weekly Wednesday night meeting that attracted more than 150 students each week last year. This all takes place in a friendly, student-oriented atmosphere," he said.

These big events combine singing, games, skits, messages, and counseling to present the Christian message "in a format designed for students," said Hankson. Students run the meetings, from planning the program to setting up chairs and acting as emcees.

Jennifer Evans, a Settlin High junior says, "Most adults don't trust kids with real responsibility, but Jeff encourages us. Besides, it's great to have somewhere fun to go where no one is getting drunk. Actually, that's what attracted me the first time. I was looking for something other than partying, and through this event, I accepted Christ."

Even parents compliment Hankson's efforts. "This meeting is really making positive changes in student," says the father of a Settlin High senior. "Not only are kids getting off the streets, but their lives are changing. My son used to be rebellious; now he *asks* how he can help around the house."

These students meet every Wednesday from 7:00 to 8:30 p.m. in the Toledo Community Church at 861 Redan Road.

For more information, call Jeff Hankson at (301) 991-0091.

Contact: (Name) _____ (Phone) _____

(Fax) _____

GETTING YOUR DUCKS IN A ROW*

Use the "storyboarding" method by writing each idea on a 4″ x 6″ card and tacking it to a board. See *The Magnet Effect* for a demonstration.

1. PURPOSE: What is one specific purpose for this outreach event?

2. TARGET: Who is the specific audience?

3. THEME: What is the specific theme?

4. GOAL: What is the specific goal?

5. IDEAS: What are the creative ideas? (At this point bring in other lay leaders on your "HIT Team." After jotting down all of the group's ideas related to your theme and goal on a separate sheet, what are the five best ones?)

6. RESOURCES: What are the specific resources you will need?

7. PRODUCTION: What will the program look like? (Use the "Program Flow Chart.")

PROGRAM

*See Chapter 7 of *The Magnet Effect* for content.

PROGRAM FLOW CHART*

Once you have worked through the "Getting Your Ducks in a Row" sheet, you will fine tune the event in this meeting with your "HIT Team" leaders. Have a typed copy of your "Getting Your Ducks in a Row" notes.

1. REVIEW. Clarify and adjust the purpose, target, theme and goal.

2. BRAINSTORM. Write your purpose, target, theme, goal, brainstorm and resources ideas on an overhead projector so you have everyone's input.

3. CREATE. Taking all you have done to this point, create the program in detail.

4. ASSIGN. Make assignments of specific responsibility to each of the "Hit Team" leaders.

5. FINE TUNE. Meet two hours before to review the program and make final adjustments.

EVENT

*See Chapter 7 of *The Magnet Effect* for content.

ENVIRONMENT EVALUATION*

COMPASSION

- Adult leaders inviting kids
  1   2   3   4   5   6   7   8   9   10
- Discipled kids prepared to bring two friends each
  1   2   3   4   5   6   7   8   9   10
- Interaction in the program
  1   2   3   4   5   6   7   8   9   10
- Individuals prayed for
  1   2   3   4   5   6   7   8   9   10

COMMUNICATION

- Barriers to non-Christians removed
  1   2   3   4   5   6   7   8   9   10

CONNECTIONS

- Students in Prayer Power Teams
  1   2   3   4   5   6   7   8   9   10
- Students prepared to bring three friends they have prayed for
  1   2   3   4   5   6   7   8   9   10
- Students trained to do follow-up
  1   2   3   4   5   6   7   8   9   10

CREATIVITY

- High-energy rowdiness time included in program
  1   2   3   4   5   6   7   8   9   10
- "Salting" of students built into the program
  1   2   3   4   5   6   7   8   9   10
- Student involvement built into the program
  1   2   3   4   5   6   7   8   9   10

CONTENT

- Program solidly based on Scripture
  1   2   3   4   5   6   7   8   9   10

ENVIRONMENT

*See Chapter 7 of *The Magnet Effect* for content.

MESSAGE PLAN*

September ————————————————————————————
Week 1
Week 2
Week 3
Week 4

October ————————————————————————————
Week 1
Week 2
Week 3
Week 4

November ————————————————————————————
Week 1
Week 2
Week 3
Week 4

December ————————————————————————————
Week 1
Week 2
Week 3
Week 4

January ————————————————————————————
Week 1
Week 2
Week 3
Week 4

February ————————————————————————————
Week 1
Week 2
Week 3
Week 4

March ————————————————————————————
Week 1
Week 2
Week 3
Week 4

April ————————————————————————————
Week 1
Week 2
Week 3
Week 4

May ————————————————————————————
Week 1
Week 2
Week 3
Week 4

*See Chapter 8 of *The Magnet Effect* for content.

RESOURCES SURVEY*

Program Element	Present Resources	Resources Needed
Crowdbreakers		
Games and Competition		
Skits		
Announcements		
Dramas		
Visual Media		
Testimonies		
Music		
Message		
Invitation		
Follow-up/Counseling		

*See Chapter 7 and 8 of *The Magnet Effect* for content.

MESSAGE RESEARCH*

1. The date of the meeting:

2. The title of the message:

3. The passage:

4. The central truth:

5. The outline of the passage:

    detailed outline

    brainstorm

    questions

    cross references

    objections

    commentaries

*See Chapter 8 of *The Magnet Effect* for content.

MESSAGE OUTLINE*

Title:

_____

The message objective:

The passage:

The outline:

Introduction

Body

<u>Points</u>	<u>Illustrations</u>	<u>Applications</u>

Conclusion

*See Chapter 8 of *The Magnet Effect* for content.

MESSAGE WRITTEN*

(Use separate sheets to write your message out,
sentence by sentence.)

Note: After you have written the message word for word, then

1. Prepare your speaking notes.
2. Practice outloud 4 or 5 times.

*See Chapter 8 of *The Magnet Effect* for content.

BIBLE RESPONSE SHEET

Date

_____

Passage

_____

Title

_____

Key verse

_____

Summary

_____

_____

_____

_____

_____

_____

_____

_____

Personal application

_____

_____

_____

_____

_____

_____

_____

_____

SAMPLE MESSAGE OUTLINE
Handling Your Parent Hassle
Luke 2:41-52

Introduction:

The way we relate to our parents determines the way we will relate to God.

Objective: To relate to our parents properly.

Body:

The Problems:

Jesus, the Son of God, lived with parents who were flawed. His parents:

1. Had a communication breakdown (vv. 43-44).
2. Panicked because of His absence (vv. 45-46).
3. Felt mistreated (v. 48).
4. Didn't understand Him (v. 50).

Identify the biggest, deepest problem you have with your parents.

The Solutions:

Make a decision to respond positively to those problems. Jesus responded properly to the problems with His parents.

1. He saw His parents' perspective (v. 41).

   Have you been rebellious toward your parents because they have not done things to suit you?

2. He set out with pure motives (vv. 46-48).

   Have your motives been to please God or to get your own way?

3. He searched for His personal identity (vv. 49-50).

   How can you learn more about who you are through your parents?

4. He submitted to His parents (v. 51).

   Have you been obedient to your parents in every way?

Determine what steps of action you will take to solve the problems with your parents.

The Results:

Because Jesus responded correctly to His parents, He matured. . .

1. Mentally–"wisdom"
2. Physically–"stature"
3. Spiritually–"favor with God"
4. Socially–"favor with man"

Conclusion:

Pray for what you want God to do in your relationship with your parents.

SAMPLE MESSAGE HANDOUT

Handling Your Parent Hassle
Luke 2:41-52

The Problems:

1.

2.

3.

4.

The biggest, deepest problem I have with my parents:

The Solutions:

1.

2.

3.

4.

The steps I will take to solve the problem with my parents:

The Results:

1.

2.

3.

4.

My prayer for what God will do in my relationship with my parents:

MESSAGE EVALUATION*

Date: _____

Message Title: _____

Text: _____

Main Point: _____

Number Attended: _____

Place: _____

	Good	Fair	Poor	Comments
Use of Scripture				
Gestures				
Pitch				
Enunciation				
Enthusiasm				
Illustrations				
Applications				
Nervous Habits				
Overuse of Words				
Other Comments				

*See Chapter 8 of *The Magnet Effect* for content.

MEETING STRUCTURE*

Event: _____

Theme: _____

Each "HIT Team" leader will be responsible for filling in the blanks for that team's area and coming to the meeting prepared to select the best idea from each category in light of the overall picture.

	Resource	Page #

- Crowd-breakers
  1.
  2.
  3.

- Games and Competition
  1.
  2.
  3.

- Skits
  1.
  2.
  3.

- Announcements
  1.
  2.
  3.

- Dramas
  1.
  2.
  3.

*See Chapter 9 of *The Magnet Effect* for content.

- Visual Media

  1.

  2.

  3.

- Testimonies

  1.

  2.

  3.

- Music

  1.

  2.

  3.

- Message

  1.

  2.

  3.

- Invitation/Follow-up/Counseling

  1.

  2.

  3.

HIT TEAM COVENANT*

"With all my heart for the Lord" (Col. 3:23)

Realizing that my friends need to know Jesus Christ and that God has challenged me to reach them, I covenant with God, my youth leaders, and other HIT Team members to:

- grow daily in my relationship with Jesus through obedience to Him
- participate in a Prayer Power Team
- prepare for and attend the weekly planning meetings
- carry out my responsibility with excellence
- participate in bringing my friends to outreach events

Signed: _____

Date: _____

*See Chapter 9 of *The Magnet Effect* for content.

PROGRAM CUE SHEET
(See sample on the next page.)

Put the entire program on one sheet.

Date: _____

Purpose: _____

Target: _____

Theme: _____

Program Overview: _____

Time	Program Item	Person

*See Chapter 9 of *The Magnet Effect* for content.

Student Impact Program Cue Sheet

Program: Insight   *Date:* Sept. 27, 1992

Revision: SHOW COPY

Program Title: "Growth"

Series Title: "FDF"

Rational: (Committed to life change) Everyone high school student here tonight can affirm that you are becoming a FDF by identifying 2 changes from within...How to see yourself...How to see others...

Purpose: The program will show....

Program Overview

Time	Overview Item Title - Person

6:30 WALK-IN MUSIC

6:41 PRELUDE
-"Somebody to Follow" - Band

6:45 WELCOME & ANNOUNCEMENTS
-Troy

-*Impact starts 10/6*
-*Impact Strategy is this Tuesday, 7pm go right to your team room or comp*
-*Insight continues next week with FDF step#3*
-*D-Team deadline is Tonight*

6:50 ATTITUDE
-Dave McCall

6:55 MESSAGE
"Growth" - Bo

7:30 SONG
"Heart's Cry" - Jodi

7:34 WORSHIP
"How you can see God changing you." - Bo & Bruce
-**In My Heart** *(you worship)*
-**Humble Thyself** *(you're humble)*
-**Casual Christian** *(you want to grow)*
-**We Are Strangers** *(you see heaven as your destiny)*

OFFERING

-**More Love** *(you want to be more like Him)*
-**Step By Step** *(you seek after Him)*

7:54 CLOSING PRAYER - BO

7:55 WALK-OUT MUSIC

SPEAKER LIGHT LEGEND
Green=ok
Yellow=5 min.
Yellow & red=1 min.
Red=over, stop

212

REHEARSAL SCHEDULE*
(See sample on the next page.)

Element	Day	Time
Crowd-breakers		
Games/Competition		
Skit		
Announcements		
Drama		
Media		
Testimonies		
Music		
Message		
Invitation/Follow-up		
Stage		
Audio		
Lights		

*See Chapter 9 of *The Magnet Effect* for content.

Schedule

Main Schedule Grid

DAY	SUNDAY										TUESDAY							
TIME	1	2	3	4	5	6	7	8	9	10	4	5	6	7	8	9	10	11
STAGE	Stage Setup			Dinner Break	Reh			Tear Down				Stage Setup	Reh					
AUDIO		Stage Setup		Dinner Break				Tear Down				Monitor Mix						
LIGHTS	Stage Setup			Diner Break				Tear Down				Stage Setup						
MEDIA	Stage Setup			Dinner Break				Tear Down				Stage Setup						
VIDEO				Rm 149 Rehearse									Stage Setup					
BAND		Corrine's Rehearse	Stage	Insight Rehearse	Break	Break						Stage Rehearsal	Break					
VOCAL		Parent's Room		Corrine's Rehearse	Break	Stage						Rory's Rehearsal	Break					
DRAMA				Rory's Rehearse								Parent's Rehearsal	Stage					
WORSHIP TEAM																		
OTHER																		

Spanning banners: **IMPACT RUN - THROUGH** and **INSIGHT RUN - THROUGH** and **INSIGHT PROGRAM** and **TEAR DOWN** (Sunday); **IMPACT RUN-THROUGH**, **IMPACT PROGRAM**, **TEAR DOWN** (Tuesday).

CREW - SUNDAY
1:00 Stage Setup
3:00 Stage Rehearsal
3:30 Run-Through
4:00 Break
5:15 Stage Rehearsal
5:30 Run-Through
6:00 Prayer
6:30 Open Doors
8:00 Teardown
9:00 Go Home

BAND - SUNDAY
1:00 Room 149
3:00 Stage Setup
3:30 Run-Through
4:00 Rehearsal
5:00 Break
5:30 Run-Through
6:00 Prayer
6:30 Open Doors
8:00 Teardown
8:30 Go Home

VOCALS - SUNDAY
1:00 Corrine's Office
3:00 Monitor Mix
3:30 Run-Through
4:00 Rehearsal
5:00 Break
5:30 Run-Through
6:00 Prayer
6:30 Open Doors
8:00 Teardown
8:30 Go Home

DRAMA - SUNDAY
1:00 Parent's Room
2:30 Stage Rehearsal
3:30 Run-Through
4:00 Go Home

WORSHIP - SUN
4:00 Corrine's Office
5:15 Monitor Mix
5:30 Run-Through
6:00 Prayer
6:30 Open Doors
8:00 Go Home

VIDEO - SUNDAY
3:00 Director
3:30 Run-Through
4:00 Break
5:30 Run-Through
6:00 Prayer
6:30 Open Doors
6:45 Program
8:00 Go Home

CREW - TUESDAY
5:30 Setup
6:30 Stage Reh.
6:45 Run-Through
7:30 Prayer
7:50 Open Doors
9:15 Teardown
11:00 Go Home

VIDEO - TUESDAY
6:00 Setup
6:45 Run-Through
7:30 Prayer
7:50 Open Doors
9:45 Go Home

BAND - TUESDAY
5:00 Rehearsal
5:45 Reh w/ Vocal
6:15 Break
6:45 Run-Through
7:30 Prayer
7:50 Open Doors
9:15 Teardown
10:00 Go Home

VOCAL - TUESDAY
5:45 Rehearsal
6:15 Break
6:45 Run-Through
7:30 Prayer
7:50 Open Doors
9:15 Clean-up
9:30 Go Home

DRAMA - TUESDAY
5:30 Rehearsal
6:15 Stage
6:45 Run-Through
7:30 Prayer
7:50 Open Doors
9:15 Clean-up
9:30 Go Home

TIME	GENERAL	AUDIO	LIGHTING	SPOTS	STAGE	BAND	MULTI-IMAGE	VIDEO
6:30 WALK-IN MUSIC								
	-curtains closed -side drapes up		-house 50%				-FDF slide up	-start recording SVHS -w. balcony video on
6:41 PRELUDE *-Somebody to Follow" - Band*								
	-open curtains							

VERSE
Oh this life, it keeps getting harder, to make it through the day
With what we have to live for, oh this life, where nothing seems to matter
And we throw our lives away, but what is there to die for?

CHORUS
All I know is that I need to find, somebody to follow

VERSE
Oh this confusion, it plagues my mind I can't think, in this sea of misdirection
My will's beginning to sink, oh this seclusion, we're building walls
Around ourselves, we won't turn to anybody, we put our trust upon shelves

CHORUS
All I know is that I need to find, somebody to follow

| TIME | GENERAL | AUDIO | TECHNICAL | | STAGE | BAND | MULTI-IMAGE | VIDEO |
			LIGHTING	SPOTS				
	VERSE Oh I'm gaining control, finding who I ought to be, like a child I've been searching And the light I now can see, oh my soul it keeps getting stronger I've finally found the answers, I'll have to search no longer **CHORUS** All I know is that I need to find, somebody to follow All I know is that I need to find, somebody to follow							
6:45	**WELCOME & ANNOUNCEMENTS** *-Troy* -Impact starts 10/6 -Impact Strategy is this Tuesday, 7pm - go right to your team room or comp -Insight continues next week with FDF step#3 *-D-Team deadline is Tonight*	-house 80%						
6:50	**ATTITUDE** *-Dave McCall* Dave: Hi, my name is Dave McCall, and I have an Attitude! *(BAND KICKS IN TO "Peter Gun")* -Band up		-band up				-Attitude slide up -slide out	

TIME	GENERAL	AUDIO	LIGHTING	SPOTS	STAGE	BAND	MULTI-IMAGE	VIDEO

6:55 MESSAGE
"Growth" - Bo

-close curtains

-keyboard intro

-FDF slide up

7:30 SONG
"Heart's Cry" - Jodi

-open curtains

-slide out

This is my heart's cry, I want to know the one who saved me and gave me life
This is my heart's cry, to be so close to Him that all my life becomes
A testimony of my Saviour's grace and love, This is my heart's cry

This is my heart's cry, much more than just a great desire-it's like a fire in me
I hear my heart cry each time I think about the cross where Jesus died
The cross should have been mine but His love broke through time
And heard my heart's cry, He heard my heart's cry

Now every other hope and dream is lost inside of this one thing
To know the one who died for me and live my life for Jesus Christ
It's my heart's cry

:05 INSTRUMENTAL

| TIME | GENERAL | TECHNICAL | | | STAGE | BAND | MULTI-IMAGE | VIDEO |
		AUDIO	LIGHTING	SPOTS				
	So let my life become a testimony of my Savior's grace and love Oh-this is my heart's cry-to stand before the Father one day And hear Him say well done-this is my heart's							

7:34 WORSHIP

"How you can see God changing you." - Bo & Bruce

-song slides

"IN MY HEART" - YOU WORSHIP

In my heart, I'm down on my knees.
In my heart, I'm down on my knees.
Right where I am, as best I can.
In my heart, I'm down on my knees.

In my heart, I bow down to You...

In my heart, I'm worshiping You...

"HUMBLE THYSELF" - YOU'RE HUMBLE

Men: Humble thyself in the sight of the Lord. (Women echo)
Men: Humble thyself in the sight of the Lord. (Women echo)

Men: And He (and He) shall lift (shall lift) you up - higher and higher.
Men: And He (and He) shall lift (shall lift) you up - up into heaven.
Men: And He (and He) shall lift (shall lift) you up.

"CASUAL CHRISTIAN" - YOU WANT TO GROW

I don't what to be, I don't want to be a casual Christian.
I don't want to live I don't want to live a lukewarm life.
'Cause I want to light up the night, with an everlasting light.
I don't want to live a casual Christian life.

© 1985 DOB Music (Division of the Forefront Communications Group, Inc.) BMI/ASCAP. ASR, ICS, CCLI, License # 4260

"WE ARE STRANGERS" - YOU SEE HEAVEN AS YOUR DESTINY

We are strangers in this land and our home lies far away.
When we get there, He'll take our hand - say "Welcome home, child, you're here to stay."

© 1986 Rick Reynoson LMP

7:47 OFFERING

"MORE LOVE" - YOU WANT TO BE MORE LIKE HIM

More love, more power, more of You in my life. (Repeat)

| TIME | GENERAL | TECHNICAL | | | | BAND | MULTI-IMAGE | VIDEO |
		AUDIO	LIGHTING	SPOTS	STAGE			
	I will worship You with all of my heart - I will worship You with all of my mind - I will worship You with all of my strength - for You are my Lord. ©1997 Mercy Publishing ASR ICS USP CCLI License ####							
	"STEP BY STEP" - YOU SEEK AFTER HIM) Oh God, You are my God, and I will ever praise You. Oh God, You are my God, and I will ever praise You. I will seek You in the morning, and I will learn to walk in Your ways. And step by step You'll lead me, and I will follow You all of my days. ©1991 Kid Brothers of St Francis Publishers ASR Edward Music Inc CCLI License ####							
7:54	**CLOSING PRAYER** *- Bo*							
7:55	**WALK-OUT MUSIC**							

220

THE PLANNING MEETINGS FLOW CHART*

Master Planning Meeting
(General plan for the year.)

Weekly Leaders' Meeting
(1. Plan ahead for the teams.
2. Set final plan for the event.)

Weekly Team Meeting
(Develop each team's plan.)

OUTREACH EVENT

*See Chapter 9 of The Magnet Effect for content.

INDIVIDUAL HIT TEAM'S PLAN*

Team: _____

Responsibility for the event: _____

Specific plan and material to carry out our responsibility:

*See Chapter 9 of *The Magnet Effect* for content.

SAMPLE HIT TEAM SIGN-UP SHEET

Telephone Team

The students who sign up for this team need to have no fear of talking to strangers. They might need some training in telephone manners.

Responsibilities:

1. Secure the telephone directories of the various schools.

2. Train the team in how to use the survey.

3. Set up a plan to distribute the numbers and make the calls. The easiest approach is to photocopy the sheets from the directories and pass them out to the team.

4. Keep accurate records. Have members of each calling team be responsible for recording the results of their calls on the central record-keeping system.

Team Sign-up:

1.   11.

2.   12.

3.   13.

4.   14.

5.   15.

6.   16.

7.   17.

8.   18.

9.   19.

10.   20.